PRINCIPALS
and STUDENT
ACHIEVEMENT

WHAT THE RESEARCH SAYS

Kathleen Cotton

Association for Supervision and Curriculum Development
Alexandria, Virginia USA

Association for Supervision and Curriculum Development
1703 N. Beauregard St. • Alexandria, VA 22311-1714 USA
Telephone: 800-933-2723 or 703-578-9600 • Fax: 703-575-5400
Web site: http://www.ascd.org • E-mail: member@ascd.org

Gene R. Carter, *Executive Director;* Nancy Modrak, *Director of Publishing;* Julie
Houtz, *Director of Book Editing & Production;* Tim Sniffin, *Project Manager;* Keith
Demmons, *Typesetter;* Eric Coyle, *Production Coordinator.*

All Web links in this book are correct as of the publication date below but
may have become inactive or otherwise modified since that time. If you
notice a deactivated or changed link, please e-mail books@ascd.org with the
words "Link Update" in the subject line. In your message, please specify the
Web link, the book title, and the page number on which the link appears.

Printed in the United States of America.

ISBN: 0-87120-827-X   ASCD product no.: 103309
ASCD member price: $18.95 nonmember price: $23.95
s10/03

Library of Congress Cataloging-in-Publication Data

Cotton, Kathleen.
   Principals and student achievement : what the research says / Kathleen
Cotton.
      p. cm.
Includes bibliographical references.
   ISBN 0-87120-827-X (alk. paper)
   1. School principals—United States. 2. Academic achievement--United
States. 3. Educational accountability--United States. I. Title.
   LB2831.93.C68 2003
   371.2'012--dc22

                                                            2003018221

13 12 11 10 09 08 07 06 05 04 03   12 11 10 9 8 7 6 5 4 3 2 1

PRINCIPALS *and* STUDENT ACHIEVEMENT

WHAT THE RESEARCH SAYS

PRINCIPALS IN THE SPOTLIGHT

OR SHOULD THE TITLE BE "PRINCIPALS ON THE SPOT"? SCHOOL REFORM has been on the agenda around the world for years. Recognition of the importance of principals, or headteachers, as they are sometimes called in European countries, to school reform has been long-standing. In the book *School Leader Development for School Improvement,* editors Blum and Butler reviewed leader development programs from eight countries and synthesized the skills and knowledge emphasized to prepare leaders for their role in leading school reform.[1] The focus on the principal as the key to the improvement of learning for all children has intensified in the past few years. The emphasis on results moves reform to a new level of accountability. It is no longer satisfactory to show that good, effective programs are being implemented in schools. The demand is for schools to show improved academic achievement for each student. Accountability for results is driving school reform in the United States, and it is central to improvement efforts in most other countries as well.

The No Child Left Behind Act (NCLB) has special meaning to principals in the United States, giving states and districts increased flexibility in how they spend their education dollars in return for setting standards for student achievement and holding educators accountable for results. The law requires or allows:

• *Accountability*. All students must meet challenging academic standards in reading and math, grades 3–8, as measured by state tests. Disaggregated data will be used to determine how well various groups of children are doing. An annual report card will make results public so parents can make more informed choices about the education of their children. There are consequences for schools that do not make adequate yearly progress.

• *Flexible spending*. Within limits, federal funds may be moved from program to program and category to category to make changes that will result in improved academic achievement for every student. The law promotes local control and decision making.

• *Parental choice*. Parents of children in low-performing schools have the right to transfer their children to better-performing schools, including public charter schools. Children in low-performing schools also have a right to supplemental educational services such as tutoring, after-school services, and summer school. Transportation to a different school and supplemental services are funded by school districts.

- *Using effective practices and programs.* The law emphasizes the use of educational programs and practices that have been demonstrated effective. Schools are expected not only to use effective programs and practices, but also to know the research supporting such practices and to justify the changes they make.[2]

While meeting the requirements of the NCLB Act takes teamwork among state, district, and school staff, the greatest pressure for change is at the school level. It all comes together in schools where students, teachers, and administrators interact in ways that result in all students meeting challenging standards. Increasingly, principals are seen as the person in the center. They are expected to make it work. And some principals have led their schools toward substantial improvement.

Leadership in an elementary school in Salem, Oregon, is an example of moving a school forward. With 94 percent of students on free or reduced-price lunch; 59 percent of the student body Hispanic, including a large percentage with limited English proficiency; and a 34 percent mobility rate, the school faced many challenges. Only 6 percent of 5th grade students met state standards in reading, 6 percent met standards in math, and 3 percent met state standards in writing when a new principal joined the staff. Four years later, 34 percent were meeting reading standards, 54 percent were meeting math standards, and 23 percent were meeting writing standards. The principal began working with staff to gain focus for the school using two basic principles, (1) no excuses will be made for student failure and (2) student learning will be at the heart of all decisions made in the school. With leadership from the principal, the staff figured out what changes would make a difference and implemented many research-based practices, including increased instructional time in key subjects, smaller groups through teaming, frequent assessment of progress, one-on-one tutoring, and more. The staff also increased their bilingual abilities and provided support for families to participate in school and help their children. The principal took the lead in finding outside resources to support needed changes, including ongoing professional development for the staff.[3]

In a quite different example of a school's progress, over a four-year period a large high school increased the number of students meeting state standards in writing from 62 to 84 percent, in reading from 42 to 52 percent, and in math problem solving from 21 to 47 percent. At the same time, American College Testing (ACT) scores increased, as did the percentage of students taking the test. The number of students earning 27 or more credits increased from 43 to 200, enrollment in Advanced Placement honors courses increased from 1,070 to 1,488, and the dropout rate went down from 7.2 to 5.7 percent. Change in this large high school took much longer than the four-year improvement in performance cited above and involved continuous effort under the leadership of three different principals. The changes made by the staff are substantial, lasting, and effective. Key changes include gaining focus on academic achievement and quality teaching; personalizing the schooling experience through a house system in which teams of teachers work with groups of students for extended time; and establishing a schedule that offers teacher planning time and flexibility for students, a career pathways system that allows students to pursue their interests and talents, and opportunities to learn in the community as well as the school. The hard, focused work over time is paying dividends for the students who attend this high school.[4]

That some principals have led their staff and communities to implement effective teaching and schooling practices to enable increasing numbers of their students, regardless of background or economic condition, to reach high levels of academic achievement brings us to this book, *Principals and Student Achievement: What the Research Says*. What principals do makes a difference.

In summarizing research on what principals in successful schools do, Kathleen Cotton describes 26 principal behaviors that contribute to student achievement. While no system of classification is perfect, the behaviors seem to fall into five categories. The first is *establishing a clear focus on student learning*, including having a vision, clear learning goals, and high expectations for learning for all students. The second is *interactions and relationships*. This category includes behaviors such as communication and interaction, emotional/interpersonal support, visibility and accessibility, and parent/community outreach and involvement. The third is *school culture*, which includes such behaviors as shared leadership/decision making, collaboration, support of risk taking, and continuous improvement. The fourth is *instruction,* which includes such behaviors as discussing instructional issues, observing classrooms and giving feedback, supporting teacher autonomy, and protecting instructional time. The fifth and final category is *accountability,* which includes monitoring progress and using student progress data for program improvement.

In addition to summarizing and describing 26 principal behaviors, Cotton reviewed and summarized research findings in other key areas, such as differences between principal leadership in elementary and secondary schools, principals in high- and low-socioeconomic schools, and gender differences.

At a time when principals are being asked to do more and be more accountable, this book provides solid information about what principals should do to improve academic achievement for all of the students they serve. As districts and schools move forward to improve academic achievement and meet the requirements of NCLB, this book will be an invaluable resource.

Robert E. Blum, Director
Center for School and District Improvement
Northwest Regional Educational Laboratory

Endnotes

1. Blum, R., & Butler, J. (Eds.) (1989). *School leader development for school improvement.* (Technical Report No. 3). International School Improvement Project. Louvain, Belgium/Amersfoort, the Netherlands: Acco Publishing.

2. U.S. Department of Education. (2002). *No child left behind: A desktop reference* (pp. 9–11). Washington, D.C.

3. Northwest Regional Educational Laboratory. (2002). *Learning by example, story 3: Highland Elementary School.* Portland, OR: Northwest Regional Educational Laboratory.

4. Northwest Regional Educational Laboratory. (2002). *Signature series: Reynolds School District.* Portland, OR: Northwest Regional Educational Laboratory.

INTRODUCTION

Our results indicate that the manner in which elementary and high school principals govern the school, build strong school climate, and organize and monitor the school's instructional program are important predictors of academic achievement.

—Ronald Heck and George Marcoulides,
"Principal Leadership Behaviors and School Achievement,"
in NASSP Bulletin

IT WOULD BE DIFFICULT TO FIND AN EDUCATIONAL RESEARCHER OR practitioner who does not believe that school principals are critically important to school success. Teachers and students know this from personal experience, and decades of research have consistently found positive relationships between principal behavior and student academic achievement. This synthesis focuses on educational research conducted from the 1970s to the present, with special emphasis on research from the past 15 years, since the latter has a great deal to say about the manner in which principals influence student performance.

Looking first at earlier research studies, we can see that two related lines of inquiry produced findings about the nature and importance of principals' influence. One is what has come to be known as the "effective schooling research," initiated by such notable figures as Ronald Edmonds, Wilbur Brookover, and Lawrence Lezotte. These researchers and those who came after them conducted studies in which high-achieving and low-achieving schools with similar student populations were examined to determine what accounted for the differences between them. With only slight variations, they repeatedly identified a common set of attributes that seemed responsible for the success of the high-achieving schools. These include strong administrative leadership, high expectations of students and staff, a safe and orderly school environment, a primary focus on learning, resources focused on achieving key objectives, regular monitoring of student learning progress, and instructional leadership on the part of the principal. Anyone familiar with the research of this period will recognize these attributes.

The second line of investigation focused primarily on the principal's involvement with the school's instructional program, identifying this involvement as the key difference between more-effective and less-effective schools. The phrase, "the principal as instructional leader," appeared in scores of research studies and reviews of the time, with different reports providing more or less detail about its meaning.

Researchers such as Kenneth Leithwood, D.J. Montgomery, and Win DeBevoise were key to this research, which produced its own list of leadership behaviors related to instruction. Principals of high-achieving schools were found to establish and gain schoolwide commitment to clear learning goals and to promote these qualities throughout their schools and communities. They engaged in "assertive, achievement-oriented leadership" (Leithwood & Montgomery, 1982, p. 334), acquiring and distributing resources as needed to meet school goals. They arranged for and often directly provided instructional improvement activities for the staff of their schools. They involved school staff and community members in decision making about school operations, and they modeled behaviors they expected from those they supervised. Their capacity for establishing positive interpersonal relationships stood them in good stead as they sought to get others focused on achieving goals, monitored classroom instruction and gave feedback, and facilitated communication internally and with constituents. Researchers contrasted these "instructional leaders" with "typical" principals, who "inevitably reported being drowned in a sea of administrivia with no time left to attend to program improvement" (Leithwood & Montgomery, p. 330).

Subsequent research has taken this important groundwork and elaborated on it. The post-1985 research offers a rich array of findings about the behaviors of effective principals and takes up other questions not addressed by earlier studies. Is the influence of principals on students direct, or is it primarily indirect—mediated through other variables, most notably teacher behavior? Do successful principals get results primarily by appealing to the self-interest of staff members, or do they somehow lead the staff to transcend self-interest to focus on the well-being of others? Are there differences between the instructional leadership behaviors of elementary and secondary principals, or between those of male and female principals? Do we need to look at the effects *on* principals' leadership—the forces that shape and limit what principals are able to do—as well as the effects *of* their leadership? The research base consulted for this report addresses these and other topics of interest for those wanting to deepen their understanding of the principal's role and influence.

The Research Base

There are many more research articles on principal effectiveness than the 81 that appear in this report's bibliography. For one thing, as mentioned previously, I focus chiefly on post-1985 research. So much of the older research goes no further than offering lists like the representative ones identified. Second, I focus only on research that looks at principals' behaviors in relation to one or more student outcomes. Thus, research that looks at the ways principals spend their time but does not relate the findings to student achievement or behavior would not be included. This report, moreover, is a representative, rather than exhaustive, summary, in which I endeavor to include the work of those researchers who are cited as experts by their peers. I trust, therefore, that I address the chief concerns and findings of key contemporary investigators of the principal's influence on student performance and related issues. Of the 81 reports I reviewed, 49 are primary documents (studies); 23 are secondary (reviews and summaries); 5 report results of both a review and a study; and 4 are not, strictly speaking, analyses of the principals' behaviors, but rather are textbook analyses, research-based guidelines, and so on. Many reports focus on more than one type of subject. All but seven of the inquiries were conducted in the United States, and more than half focus on low-SES (socioeconomic status) minority students. The subjects of the 81 reports are as follows:

- Elementary students: 25 reports
- Middle or secondary students: 9 reports
- Both elementary and secondary or an unspecified "general" student subject pool: 35 reports
- Teachers and students: 11 reports
- Principals and students: 7 reports
- Students, teachers, and principals: 11 reports
- Teachers and principals: 6 reports
- Teachers only: 2 reports
- Principals only: 3 reports
- Different combinations of students, parents, teachers, school board members, community members, and superintendents: 6 reports

Many reports are also concerned with more than one outcome area. The areas the research addresses are as follows:

- Student achievement (in general or in specified subject areas): 56 reports
- Student attitudes (toward school, learning, self as learner, teachers, and peers): 10 reports
- Student behavior (discipline, extracurricular participation): 8 reports
- Teacher attitudes: 15 reports
- Teacher behavior: 4 reports
- Dropouts: 3 reports
- Others (attitudes of parents, principals, school board members, and so forth): 3 reports

The studies exhibit many different kinds of research designs. Most surveyed teachers from high-achieving schools about the behavior of their principals, surveyed principals of high-achieving schools about their own behavior, or relied on researcher observations or analyses (e.g., of time use).

RESEARCH FINDINGS ABOUT PRINCIPAL BEHAVIORS AND STUDENT ACHIEVEMENT

THE PRINCIPAL CHARACTERISTICS AND BEHAVIORS INVESTIGATED AND what the researchers found are the focus of most of this report. Though I address them one at a time to provide as much detail as possible about each one, in the real world they do not exist separately, and none of the researchers suggest that they do. On the contrary, the extraordinary principals who are the focus of some of these studies embody all or nearly all these traits and actions. And as we shall see, the picture that emerges of their effectiveness is much more than a mere collection of behaviors.

Safe and Orderly School Environment

From the earliest research to the present day, the principal's establishment and maintenance of a safe, orderly school environment has been identified as the most fundamental element of effectiveness. Effective principals bring about this kind of environment by exhibiting personal warmth and accessibility, ensuring that there is broad-based agreement about standards for student behavior, communicating high behavioral standards to students, seeking input from students about behavior policies, applying rules consistently from day to day and from student to student, delegating disciplinary authority to teachers, and providing in-school suspension accompanied by support for seriously disruptive students.[1]

In their review of the effective schooling research, Sammons, Hillman, and Mortimore found that "effective discipline involves keeping good order, consistently enforcing fair, clear and well-understood rules and infrequent use of actual punishment" (1995, p. 19). The school researcher-observers in Scheurich's 1998 study report similar findings regarding the high-achieving schools they scrutinized:

> For these schools, discipline cases are rare . . . .
> Discipline or order, as traditionally construed, is not the focus. The focus is on embedding an understanding of appropriate conduct (conduct that applies fairly and equally, even lovingly, to both adults and children) into the organizational culture of the school itself. (pp. 473–474)

And in their recent study of nine high-performing, high-poverty urban elementary schools, Johnson and Asera (1999) found that school leaders

> fostered in students a sense of responsibility for appropriate behavior and they created an environment in which students were likely to behave well. Discipline problems became rare as the schools implemented multi-faceted approaches for helping students learn responsibility for their own behavior. (p. 3)

Vision and Goals Focused on High Levels of Student Learning

Decades of research have found that a principal's strong focus on academics is a key determinant of school achievement outcomes.[2] One expression of such a focus is the principal's frequent emphasis to all who hold a stake in the school that learning is the most important purpose of schooling. Another is to reach out to stakeholders to help shape and support the school's goals. The principal also expresses it by allocating generous amounts of time to pursuing reading and mathematics objectives; communicating the expectation of high learning for all students; and insisting that mission statements, slogans, mottoes, and displays emphasizing the school's academic goals are visible around the school. Principals of high-achieving schools also evaluate "all proposals for change in terms of their potential for enhancing student learning" (Cotton, 2000, p. 10).

The critical importance of this finding, together with the richness and depth of detail about it, is expressed in the reports of key researchers. Scheurich's 1998 investigation determined that

> these successful schools and their leadership do not just have a strong vision, they have a particular vision, . . . driven by their passionate commitment to their belief that there are ways to do schooling so that literally all children do well. (p. 468)

Mendez-Morse (1991) also notes that principals

> have a vision—a picture of what they want students to achieve. They engage teachers, parents, students and others to share in creating the vision. They encourage them to join in the efforts to make that vision a reality. They keep the vision in the forefront. (p. 2)

A study of shared decision making in 24 schools found that, in the successful schools, "principals and other school leaders talked enthusiastically and engagingly about what the school stands for in language that all stakeholders could understand" and that they

> used multiple approaches to developing, communicating, and applying an educational vision. Sometimes the

vision for the school was part of a mission statement, statement of beliefs, or slogans—but leaders were able to tell people what they stand for. (Peterson, Gok, & Warren, 1995, p. 5)

Based on his 1992 research review of the relationship among motivation, school culture, and student achievement, Renchler recommends that principals "work with students, teachers, parents, and others to establish challenging but achievable school goals that promote academic achievement and the motivation that goes with it" (p. 28). According to Johnson and Asera's 1999 study of successful urban minority schools,

school leaders identified and pursued an important, visible, yet attainable first goal. They focused on the attainment of this first goal, achieved success, and then used their success to move toward more ambitious goals. (p. 3)

High Expectations for Student Learning

The principal's expression of high expectations for students is part of the vision that guides high-achieving schools and is a critical component in its own right. Researchers from Edmonds to the present have consistently found that high-achieving schools (including poor and minority schools) are successful in part because the principals communicate to

everyone in the school their expectations of high performance. Butler (1997), whose previously low-performing, poor,
minority school became high achieving under her direction,
addresses the importance of these high expectations:

> There is nothing that will improve a student's self-esteem
> better than academic success. Engineering such success
> . . . is a good teacher's obligation. But lowering the bar
> so that anyone can step over it does not create a gen-
> uine feeling of success. It is patronizing, artificial, and
> demoralizing. (p. 30)

There is widespread agreement that having genuinely high
expectations is a vital component of school success.[3] But
Scheurich is careful to point out that, contrary to what some
seem to think, having high expectations of children does
not mean making harsh demands on them. He writes that
many proponents of school improvement have emphasized
high expectations, but often

> the belief is that high expectations remedy the supposed
> deficits that the children bring to school with them and
> the negative effects of low teacher expectations for some
> children. There is, also, a kind of harshness that some-
> times accompanies this—that children should not be
> coddled or spoiled but should be pushed to achieve or
> taught the discipline of achievement. In contrast, in these

highly successful schools, the focus on high expectations is based on the revolutionary belief that the natural condition of all children is high performance . . . and that this high performance is not based on pushing children but on providing loving, facilitating conditions that deliver learning in a way that fits, supports, engages, and energizes the child. (pp. 460–461)

Self-Confidence, Responsibility, and Perseverance

Scheurich goes on to say that, in the high-achieving schools he studied, "the administrator holds herself or himself accountable for the success of the whole school" (p. 475). Other researchers make the same point.[4] Chase and Kane's 1983 review found that these principals have "confidence in their ability to take action and influence situations" (p. 15), and Wagstaff and colleagues (1998) found that the principals in the high-performing, predominantly African American schools they studied shared a "'no excuses' attitude about student performance" (p. 14).

Not that success necessarily comes easily. According to Johnson and Asera's study, the principals in high-achieving schools succeeded because they believed in themselves *and* "persisted through difficulties, setbacks, and failures. In spite of challenges and frustrations, school leaders did not stop trying to improve their schools" (1999, p. 3).

Visibility and Accessibility

In high-achieving schools, the principals do not spend their time cloistered in their offices, keeping company with administrivia. On the contrary, the researchers[5] find them to be unvaryingly present and approachable in the everyday life of the school. Black finds that they "maintain an accessible and inviting office" (1997, p. 5) and that they use humor to help others feel comfortable in their presence (p. 7). Perhaps most important, these effective principals are a frequent presence in classrooms, observing and interacting with teachers and students, a point I shall return to later in this report.

Positive and Supportive School Climate

The principal's contribution to the quality of the school climate is arguably a composite of all the things he or she says or does. But because climate is so often singled out as a key feature of high-achieving schools, findings that specifically connect principals' climate-enhancing behaviors with student performance are identified here.[6] According to Steller's 1988 summary of the behaviors of effective principals, forming an academic climate is one of their main contributions to their school's success:

> Effective principals create a school climate where academic achievement is the primary goal. And policies and procedures are instituted to achieve that goal. In addi-

tion, effective principals provide the administrative support that allows teachers to concentrate on this primary goal. (p. 21)

In her 1990 study of "outstanding secondary principals," Bartell describes the sort of social climate observed in these high-achieving schools:

Certain themes about effective schooling emerged from these discussions. An effective school has a positive school climate. Students feel good about attending such a school and teachers feel good about teaching there. The entire staff works together to foster a caring attitude. (p. 126)

Larsen's 1987 study of high- and low-achieving schools defines school climate as "the norms, expectations and beliefs of the people within a school which govern their behavior in the domain of student achievement" (p. 15). By this definition, he finds the principal's positive contributions to the school climate to be critical to school success.

Elements that build a positive school climate are also addressed individually in the sections that follow.

Communication and Interaction

As one principal advised, "Put people before paper" (Stolp, 1991, p. 4). Researchers consistently find a positive relationship between principals' human interaction and communication skills on the one hand, and the success of their students on the other.[7] Effective principals not only share information, but they also listen and take the suggestions of staff and constituents seriously, acknowledging that they do not have all the answers. Black finds that successful principals conduct vigorous outreach activities to engage all concerned in discourse about the school.

Gaziel's 1995 study comparing the principals of high-achieving and average Israeli schools concludes that "the core element of the principal's work is primarily verbal communication. This is both interpersonal and informational, for it depends on human relationships and a flow of information" (p. 186). Wendel, Hoke, and Joekel (1996) find that successful administrators whom they profile use communication skills to build close relationships and use relationships to extend communication patterns. These administrators work to improve their oral and written communication skills, value others' ideas and feedback, and work to improve their listening skills (p. 155). When hiring new staff, they seek people with good communication skills (p. 164). One could cite many more examples from the research, including some that address the *absence* of these critical skills. Davis (1998), after identifying critical principal attributes and behaviors, writes,

> The concept that effective principals must have good people skills is so obvious that it may seem needlessly redundant to make further comment. However, if it was that obvious, then why would over 65 percent of the superintendents who responded to [one survey] com-

ment that poor interpersonal skills was the No. 1 reasons why principals lose their jobs? (p. 9)

Emotional and Interpersonal Support

Researchers tell us that principals of high-achieving schools are capable and caring communicators in the interpersonal sphere as well as in the public and task-oriented domains.[8] Evans and Teddlie's 1995 review found that principals who were effective in facilitating positive change in their schools provided "both emotional and practical support" (p. 5) to those around them. DeBevoise's 1984 summary identifies the provision of "emotional support and incentive for teachers" (p. 19) as a key practice of effective principals.

Valentine and Bowman, in their 1991 study, found that principals of recognized high-performing schools were distinguishable from principals of randomly selected schools based, in part, on scores they received in the interpersonal realm. Specifically, they received higher marks for their "ability to foster positive interpersonal relationships" and their "effective communication." They were sensitive to teachers' needs, giving them support and reinforcement. They also got high marks for their "communication, encouragement, support, and high visibility" with students and their practice of "encouraging expression of feelings, opinions, pride, loyalty through team management, sensitivity, humor, and personal example" (p. 3). Not surprisingly, trust is frequently identified as a key component of these personal communications (e.g., in Gullatt & Lofton, 1996, and Riordan & da Costa, 1998).

Parent and Community Outreach and Involvement

We have known for a long time that there is a significant and positive relationship between parents' active participation in their children's learning and the children's academic performance. So it is not surprising to learn that principals of high-achieving schools are more involved in outreach to parents and other community members than are less-successful principals.[9] Effective principals interact with parents and the community to communicate their vision for their school, get constituent input, and make certain that the resulting goals are broadly understood. They engage parents and community members as classroom helpers, take meetings to neighborhoods, arrange for teachers to ride school buses in order to meet parents, have schools serve as community centers, and encourage parents to work with their children on instructional activities in the home.

Bartell's study found that "outstanding" principals routinely solicit input from parents and community members for decision making (p. 125). Davis's review found that principals of higher-achieving schools had higher levels of parent and community satisfaction (p. 8). Gaziel's study of principals' use of time found that the principals of the high-performing schools devoted 66 percent more of their work time on parent and community relationships than did the principals of the average schools (p. 184). Johnson and Asera describe the strategy used by the principals of the high-performing inner-city minority schools in their study:

> Educators made efforts to win the confidence and respect of parents, primarily by improving the achievement of students. Then educators built strong partnerships with parents in support of student achievement. (p. 3)

Scheurich's study sums up the attitude of leaders of the successful schools:

> The school exists for and serves the community—there is little separation. . . . These schools see parents and themselves as collaborators in the education of the children, and so the schools do everything they can to positively promote this collaboration. . . . No matter what the education or income level of the parents, the school staff treat all of the parents with respect, appreciation, warmth, sensitivity, and care. (p. 467)

Rituals, Ceremonies, and Other Symbolic Actions

Researchers tell us that the symbolic actions principals take are correlated with student results. Ceremonies and rituals intended to honor tradition, instill pride, recognize excellence, and stimulate proprietary interest in the school as a collective endeavor are integral to effective schools and are often missing—or are curiously hollow—in less effective ones. Such events strengthen staff and student affiliation with the school and mobilize their energy in support of its continued improvement, thus maintaining and deepening its culture. In his 1991 ERIC summary addressing the relationship among leadership, school culture, and student achievement, Stolp writes that culture includes

> the historically transmitted patterns of meaning that include the norms, values, beliefs, ceremonies, rituals, traditions, and myths understood . . . by members of the school community. This system of meaning often shapes what people think and how they act. (p. 2)

The effective principals in Black's 1997 review were found to "nurture traditions, rituals, ceremonies, and symbols that reinforce the school's culture" and to "organize and support ceremonies that honor past traditions and create new ones" (p. 33). As part of what Manasse (1984) calls their "purposing" behavior, the effective principals in her study were found to

> pay close attention to the issues on which people agree, and use rituals, symbols, slogans, and selective centralization to hold the system together. To manage symbols effectively, they spend a lot of time one-on-one, constantly reminding people of the central vision, monitoring its

application, and teaching people to interpret what they are doing in common language." (p. 46)

The inspirational force of these actions comes from their use in the service of an important goal, without which they cannot capture and hold the imagination of those the principal hopes to lead. When they *are* aligned with worthy goals for students, these "cultural mechanisms," as they are called in Leitner's 1994 study—and particularly "stories, icons and rituals"—can "influence teacher behavior" by activating their sense of attachment and loyalty to the school (p. 224).

Shared Leadership, Decision Making, and Staff Empowerment

A large and growing volume of research repeatedly finds that, when principals empower their staffs through sharing leadership and decision-making authority with them, everyone benefits, including students. In the research examined for this report, principals of high-achieving schools involved their staffs in school governance and instructional program decisions.[10]

Blase and Blase's study (1994) of teacher empowerment finds that "successful principals were those whose staffs had attained high levels of empowerment and participative decision making" (p. 12). The need for shared decision making emerges, not only from the prosaic truism that "many heads are better than one," but also from the reality that there are simply too many decisions in a typical school for one person to handle effectively. Upon studying the time-use patterns of highly successful and average principals, Gaziel concludes that

> the excessive work load, with the variety of activities, the mixture of external and internal concerns, the range of people encountered, and the dominance of information transmission involved in the work, indicates that the principal should adopt a team managerial view. He or she cannot run the organization alone. The delegation of authority can help in overcoming interruptions and the excessive workload, as indicated by the distribution of time of the principals at high-performing schools as opposed to that of the principals at average schools. (pp. 188–189)

Cotton (1992) and Gullatt and Lofton (1996) find that for school-based management structures to be effective, teachers need to have increased authority to make decisions concerning matters of curriculum and instruction. Cotton's review also found that site teams need real decision-making authority (as opposed to being merely advisory); should have information about legal requirements, budgets, and other matters that affect their decisions; and require training in problem solving, conflict resolution, consensus building, and so on. In summarizing findings from a study of 24 schools implementing shared decision-making structures,

Peterson, Gok, and Warren (1995) write,

> In short, for decentralized, shared decision making to be successful school leadership needs, first to be able to articulate a shared educational vision for the school so that the new governance structures can have some clarity of purpose and direction. Second, schools with SBDM [site-based decision making] need to have leaders with knowledge and skills in governance and decision making. Third, they need the ability to develop effective working teams. (p. 1)

Collaboration

Closely related to the benefits of shared decision making are the researchers' discoveries about the positive outcomes that emerge when principals and others establish and maintain a truly collaborative school culture.[11] In such a culture, schooling is "deprivatized," and there is a norm of principal, teachers, and others learning and planning and working together to upgrade their skills and knowledge and improve their school. The principals in Evans and Teddlie's instructionally effective schools were found to "create collaborative working arrangements" (p. 3), while their less-effective counterparts did not. Likewise, in Johnson and Asera's high-performing, low-SES schools, the principal structured the day "to ensure that collaboration around instructional issues became an important part of the school day and the school week" (p. 3). Thomas's (1997) review of management styles in relation to school effectiveness found that

> the leadership style which had the greatest impact on teacher morale was collaborative. This new leadership role of the principal has also resulted in a need for teachers to accept increased responsibility for leadership within the schools. Involving the staff in decisions affected the development of a collaborative school climate which according to findings shows a statistical relationship between teacher morale and students' achievements. (p. 35)

As some writers have noted, "collaborative" refers to both a manner of approaching tasks and the feeling of solidarity that accompanies it. The schools led by Scheurich's effective principals were found to exhibit both the sentiment and the style: "Virtually all the staff have bonded together in a deep way so that they feel they are doing the work of schooling together, as a family" (p. 470).

Though collaboration among educators in schools undeniably supports both teacher morale and student achievement, it is not as widespread as one would hope. Riordan and da Costa, in their 1998 report of five studies on leadership and collaboration, observe that many studies "have reported that a lack of administrative support and the absence of time explains why collaborative relations are not more common among workers in schools" (p. 1).

Efforts to promote greater administrative support of collaboration would nevertheless be well advised since, according to Wendel, Hoke, and Joekel's study of outstanding principals, "successful school administrators recognize the need for innovation, change, and continuous improvement through collaborative efforts to enhance teaching and learning" (p. 128).

Some General Findings about Instructional Leadership

To reflect contemporary interest in the principal's instructional role, in the following sections of this report, I focus more intensely on instructional matters. Again, because principals' actions do not exist in isolation from one another, there will be some overlap with information presented in earlier sections.

"Effective principals are at the center of curricular and instructional improvements within their schools," writes Steller (p. 16), and hundreds of research studies corroborate this assertion. Since the beginning of research about principals' impact on student results, studies have shown that principals who are knowledgeable about and actively involved with their school's instructional program have higher-achieving students than principals who manage only the noninstructional aspects of their schools.[12] Early researchers found that

> principals of effective schools were more concerned about instruction and communicated their views about it; the principals assumed responsibility for instructional decisions, coordinated instructional programs, and emphasized academic standards. (Wellisch et al., 1978, quoted in Walberg & Lane, 1985)

In short, principals of high-performing schools "support and facilitate instruction in every way possible," as Bartell puts it (1990, p. 122).

What are these ways? The research focuses on elements such as the following:

- Continually pursuing high levels of student learning
- Establishing a norm of continuous improvement
- Facilitating discussion of instructional issues
- Observing classrooms frequently and providing feedback to teachers
- Respecting teacher autonomy
- Protecting instructional time
- Supporting teachers' risk taking
- Providing staff development opportunities and activities
- Supplying other resources, such as time and materials
- Monitoring student progress and reporting findings
- Using student achievement data to improve programs
- Recognizing student and teacher achievement
- Role modeling

These will be discussed in the sections that follow.

Ongoing Pursuit of High Levels of Student Learning

Beyond establishing a vision, setting goals, and reinforcing them in symbolic ways, effective principals remain focused on achieving high levels of student learning and provide resources and even pressure to keep others similarly focused.[13] They always strive to improve the achievement and general well-being of the students in their schools. In concert with staff members, the principals in the high-performing urban minority schools in Johnson and Asera's research

> aligned instruction to the standards and assessments required by the state or the school district. Teachers and administrators worked together to understand precisely what students were expected to know and be able to do. Then, they planned instruction to ensure that students would have an excellent chance to learn what was expected of them. (p. 3)

These principals "constantly challenged teachers and students to higher levels of academic attainment" (p. 3). Peterson, Gok, and Warren find that effective principals, in their work with site teams, "developed a systematic process for planning, problem solving, and decision making that was focused on school improvement." In so doing, they headed off the teams' tendency "to focus on management and administrivia rather than instructional improvement" (p. 6). Sagor's 1992 case study finds that the successful principals demonstrated "a constant push for improvement, . . . the right combination of pressure to improve, along with meaningful support for the improvement initiatives themselves" (p. 13).

Steller's 1988 research review concludes that "the effective principal's instructional leadership has a singular thrust—to ensure that all students learn" (p. 18), and it describes the actions principals take to realize that goal. In Scheurich's high-performing schools:

> The pedagogy, the curriculum, the organization of the school itself, the conduct of students and staff, parent involvement, and staff development—all aspects of schooling—are driven by whatever it takes to achieve high levels of academic success and a positive, healthy environment for all students. (pp. 461–462)

In general, these principals do not stop with encouraging and facilitating high levels of student learning; they insist on it and push unrelentingly. The Reavis, Vinson, and Fox case study principal is a good example. In addition to a "constant emphasis on high achievement," he saw to it that teachers who resisted the high-success culture "were 'pestered' until they transferred, quit, or resigned" (p. 200).

By way of a counter-example, in Sammons, Hillman, and Mortimore's comparison study of high-, low-, and average-performing schools,

> schools in the less effective group acknowledged that, in the past, too little emphasis had been placed on student

achievement, and it was recognised that considerable efforts to raise teachers' and pupils' expectations and emphasise the school's teaching/learning functions were needed. (p. 306)

Norm of Continuous Improvement

Given the principals' intense interest in promoting learning gains, it is not surprising that the schools are characterized not only by high achievement, but also by a norm of continuous improvement.[14] Under their leadership, staff members have a matter-of-fact expectation that improvement is a permanent part of school life and act accordingly.

The critical importance of establishing such a norm has been found by researchers since the early days of the principal-as-instructional-leader research. The research reviewed by Chase and Kane established that effective principals have "a view of instructional improvement as an ongoing process" (p. 15), and both DeBevoise and Leithwood and Montgomery published similar findings. This has not changed. Under the direction of the highly effective principals studied by Bartell, the schools are "dynamic and changing, constantly striving to do better" (p. 126), and McCallum's 1999 study of literacy in four effective schools found them to be characterized by "a culture of 'making things better' " (p. 21).

Discussion of Instructional Issues

Researchers tell us that principals of high-achieving schools are knowledgeable about curriculum and instruction, facilitate discussion among staff about these issues, and engage in this discourse themselves.[15] In fact, all the Ronald Heck studies I consulted found "promoting discussion of instruction" to be among the top three or four most important things principals do. Johnson and Asera's research found that

> school leaders created opportunities for teachers to work, plan, and learn together around instructional issues. Time was structured to ensure that collaboration around instructional issues became an important part of the school day and the school week. (p. 3)

Bamburg and Andrews (1991) found that effective principals made themselves accessible to discuss instruction and participated in staff development activities focused on instruction (p. 188). Larsen's 1987 study notes that they participate both in formal and informal discussions concerning instruction as it affects student achievement. And according to Sagor, they "continually ask [teachers] probing questions about curriculum and instruction" (p. 18).

High and Achilles (1986) identified a kind of quid pro quo in the successfully run schools they studied: "The principal involves teachers in school decision making and expects to be involved in individual classroom decision making" (p. 20).

Classroom Observation and Feedback to Teachers

Apropos of that last point, researchers have identified a link between principals' classroom observation and feedback to teachers on the one hand, and student academic perform-ance on the other.[16] Principals of high-achieving schools do not visit classrooms just for social reasons, nor do they appear only at evaluation time. Instead, they study teachers' instructional approaches, take their turn at delivering instruction, and follow up with feedback to and mutual planning with teachers. Heck (1992) found that "the amount of time principals spend directly observing class-room practices was one of the three most important predic-tors of student achievement" (p. 30). Larsen's study found that, in an instructionally effective school, "the principal makes regular visits to the classrooms" (p. 14). Likewise, Mendez-Morse found that in high-performing, predomi-nantly minority, low-SES schools, "principals frequently visit classrooms for instructional purposes" (p. 3). And the lofty goal of the effective principals studied by Sagor is that they "try to visit each classroom every day" (p. 19).

Nor do effective principals "wing it" in their assessments of teaching. Instead, like the principals in Bartell's study, many participate in "extensive training programs . . . to increase their own skills in performance evaluation" (p. 123).

Support of Teacher Autonomy

The research on principals of high-performing schools finds that they are more involved in teachers' instructional practices, *yet at the same time* they allow teachers more instructional autonomy than principals do in less-effective schools. This seeming contradiction resolves itself when we examine the nature of the principals' involvement and the teachers' autonomy. In these high-performing schools, the principals take a greater interest in instruction and add their voices to the discourse about it—in groups and one-on-one with teachers. This increases their understanding of the instructional issues teachers face and renders them much more useful in working with teachers, as equals, to resolve such issues.

At the same time, these principals respect their teachers' judgment and, knowing that the teachers are continually engaged with other staff in learning activities regarding instruction, allow them great latitude to teach as they see fit. In the conclusion to their study of administrator behaviors and student achievement, Firestone and Wilson (1989) write,

> With regard to the question of what principals can do to contribute to student achievement, this study reinforces the

> view that principals contribute most by supporting teach-
> ers' efforts . . . and giving them autonomy to adjust to in-
> class and over-time variation in student ability. (p. 24)

Heck and Marcoulides (1993) put it more tersely, reporting that principals enhance student achievement by "leaving teachers alone to teach" (p. 25). Reitzug's trenchant criticism (1997) of textbooks on supervision calls for principals to

> shed the telling-and-prescribing orientation that charac-
> terizes their role in currently dominant supervision mod-
> els. Instead, principals must focus on asking questions
> that facilitate the examination of practice. (p. 342)

Reitzug also notes that one way a supportive environment for teaching can be developed is by "providing teachers and staff greater autonomy" (p. 342). Finally, Wendel, Hoke, and Joekel conclude their report with the observation that, along with pursuing excellence and upholding quality of educa-tion for all, the other action that administrators can take is "to provide instructional autonomy to teachers" (p. 43).

Effective principals also enhance teacher autonomy by shielding staff from excessive intrusions or pressure exerted by forces outside the school.[17] Recognizing that staff cannot work effectively if they are overly scrutinized and critiqued, effective principals "protect staff from external pressures and interference from the community and the central office" (Gullatt & Lofton, 1996, pp. 20–21).

Support of Risk Taking

A natural extension of principals' respect and protection of teacher autonomy is the encouragement they give to take risks—to try to improve the effectiveness of instruction through experimenting with different kinds of lessons or new approaches to teaching. Principals of high-achieving schools are described in the research literature as supporters of teacher innovation who understand and accept that some new ideas will work and some will not.[18]

Successful principals in Sagor's case study differed in many ways, but all viewed teaching "as an experimental science" (p. 18) and therefore encouraged innovation. In the schools headed by Scheurich's effective administrators, innovation is encouraged, and "if the experiment does not work, no one is blamed. It is simply dropped and [school staff] move on to another new possibility" (p. 472). They took the view that "some experiments fail and that's OK" (p. 470). Reitzug quotes Linda Darling-Hammond and Milbrey McLaughlin as saying that principals need to "create and sustain settings in which teachers feel safe to admit mistakes, to try (and possibly fail)" (p. 341). In describing her own successful approach, Butler writes, "I consistently let the teachers know that I supported their risk taking" (p. 31).

Perhaps the principals of high-achieving schools encourage teachers to take risks because they tend to be risk takers themselves. Wendel, Hoke, and Joekel note that the outstanding principals they studied not only support "experimentation and staff growth" (p. 128), but that they

> all attribute their success to their willingness and ability to take calculated risks. In virtually every case, however, they stated clearly that their wanting to take risks was for the benefit of students, staff, district, or community. (p. 137)

A good example of this sort of purposeful risk taking is reported by researcher Barbara Sizemore, who looked at the behaviors of principals of high-achieving, low-SES, predominantly African American schools. Sizemore (1985) found that these principals were willing to challenge the normative attitudes and practices of others in the school system by insisting, for example, that their students are capable of high learning and putting in place organizational and instructional practices that enhance learning.

Professional Development Opportunities and Resources

The research attributes much of the principals' success to the professional development opportunities that they provide for their staff members, particularly the teaching staff.[19] The successful principals offered not only more activities but also a wider range of them, both in terms of structure and content, than less successful ones did. Opportunities included in-school activities provided by principals or staff members, group learning sessions like those described in the learning organization literature, district-sponsored events, off-site workshops and conferences, and college coursework.

Content ranged from general to subject-specific pedagogical skills, subject-area content, and process skills such as decision making and problem solving. In addition to arranging for the activities, principals took part in many of them and "learned how training content was to be used in the classroom" (Wagstaff, Melton, Lasless, & Combs, 1998, p. 21).

Gaziel's time-use study says it all: "For the average-school principals the main time use was desk work. For the high-performing-school principals the largest amount of time was spent on professional development" (p. 185).

Effective principals were creative in finding ways to secure the resources necessary to make professional development opportunities available. In fact, principals of high-achieving schools are adept at finding and providing resources—financial, human, time, materials, and facilities—for all kinds of instruction-related needs.[20] Chase and Kane's review found that effective principals had "the ability to secure and allocate resources in ways that support appropriate staff and student behavior" (p. 15). Gurr (1997), summarizing the work of Peter Hill, notes that successful principals are skilled at "acquiring appropriate resources and facilities" (p. 7). Johnson and Asera report that

> School leaders got the resources and training that teach-
> ers perceived they needed to get their students to achieve
> at high levels. In particular, school leaders made sure
> that teachers felt like they had adequate materials,
> equipment, and professional development. (p. 3)

Levine and Levine (2000, p. 10) found that the actions principals take to make school improvement "doable and man-
ageable" are also important resources. Such actions include
(1) providing "specific guidelines and procedures" for teachers to use in implementing new activities and (2) deploying
staff creatively so as to keep classes as small as possible and
make instructional assistance available to teachers on a daily
basis. These kinds of resources smooth the way for staff as
they work to turn improvement plans into reality.

Protecting Instructional Time

Research shows that in many schools, considerable instructional time is lost to excessive loudspeaker announcements
and other administrative intrusions, too-frequent assemblies
and other all-school gatherings, and additional elements over
which the principal has total or partial control. Such losses
are then reflected in the lower performance of students in
those schools. Principals of effective schools, on the other
hand, are careful to protect instructional time and to arrange
for additional instructional time outside the regular school
day as needed.[21] Bartell's subjects were found to "establish

rules, guidelines, and operational procedures to insure instructional time is protected" (1990, p. 195). Evans and Teddlie's review also noted that effective principals "allocate and protect instructional time" (1995, p. 2). Johnson and Asera comment on a strategy used by principals of urban minority schools to improve student learning:

> School leaders created additional time for instruction. In some cases, efforts focused on creating additional time for attention to critical instructional issues during the school day. In other cases, efforts focused on creating additional time beyond the regular school day. (p. 3)

Monitoring Student Progress and Sharing Findings .

Edmonds, Brookover and Lezotte, and other pioneering researchers identified the frequent and careful monitoring of student academic progress as one of the half-dozen or so major attributes of effective principals and their schools. Subsequent researchers have repeatedly confirmed the importance of this practice.[22] Monitoring included both those efforts personally conducted by the administrative staff and those the principal took to ensure that teachers were tracking their students' learning.

"The principal ensures that systematic procedures for monitoring student progress are utilized by staff" (1987, p. 14),

Larsen writes of the principals of instructionally effective schools. In addition, effective principals of culturally or socio-economically diverse schools are careful to disaggregate achievement data so as to determine the performance and needs of particular groups. Wagstaff and his colleagues found that, in the high-performing, largely African American district he studied, "disaggregation of standardized test data was common practice" (1998, p. 21).

These successful principals also establish procedures for disseminating the results to parents and community members. For example, Gullatt and Lofton's review of the principal's role in promoting academic gains includes the finding that the effective administrator "communicates data about student progress to the community" (p. 27), and the analysis of Heck, Larsen, and Marcoulides (1990) supports this as well.

Use of Student Progress Data for Program Improvement

Successful principals not only monitor and report student progress data, but they also ensure that findings are used to improve the instructional program.[23] Bartell found that they know how to interpret student performance data, and they review and use it as a basis for plans for improvement (p. 125). The principals in the Mendez-Morse review were found to "use data to focus attention on improving the curriculum or instructional approach to maximize student achievement . . . and to determine staff development activities that strengthen teachers' instructional skills" (p. 3).

Butler directed her staff to use student performance data creatively: "All teachers would examine data on their students' achievement, and areas of greatest need would be linked to areas of greatest strength as a means of remediating weakness" (p. 30). The successful principals studied by Levine and Levine (2000) redeployed staff and provided professional development activities focused on classroom arrangements and instructional strategies and resources for helping low achievers (p. 5).

But monitoring progress and utilizing data are not about addressing needs only. Johnson and Asera's principals also "used data to identify, acknowledge, and celebrate strengths" (p. 3).

Recognition of Student and Staff Achievement

As for celebrating strengths, principals of high-achieving schools make a point of recognizing achievement and improvement on the part of students and, through them, of staff.[24] Such recognition, when public and formalized, is one of the symbolic rituals that enhance affiliation with the school and help to fortify its identity. In Reavis, Vinson, and Fox's 1999 case study, the principal gave both formal and informal recognition of teachers for their students' successes and of students for achievement, improvement, and effort (p. 201).

Sammons, Hillman, and Mortimore's review found that "school-wide or public recognition of academic success and of other aspects of positive behavior contribute to effectiveness" (1995, p. 19). Short and Spencer's 1990 study identified a positive correlation between principals' visibility and recognition of student accomplishments on the one hand, and student motivation and classroom engagement on the other (p. 120). And Scarnati's finding is that "increased recognition is one of the greatest motivators available, and is often the key to high staff morale" (1994, p. 79).

Role Modeling

As indicated earlier, many of the reviewed studies utilized teacher surveys to gather information about principals in high-achieving schools. In their descriptions of their principals' styles and approaches, the teachers' admiration for the principals' leadership comes through. As highly as the teachers—and the researchers—esteem the principals' conduct in these areas, however, what the staff clearly admire most is that their principals "walk their talk," serving as valuable role models for the behaviors they seek to instill in others.[25]

Principals received high marks, for example, for their participation in the professional development activities they arranged for their staffs. Bamburg and Andrews find that, in contrast with the principals of low-achieving schools, successful principals participated in these activities, in keeping with the finding that "the principal's participation and involvement in staff development is a powerful factor in the successful adoption and implementation of curriculum innovations" (p. 188). Wagstaff and his colleagues note that such principals joined in professional development sessions with their staffs (p. 21), and Wendel, Hoke, and Joekel found that "successful administrators know the value of continuous professional development [and] offer no excuses for looking for additional ways to improve their leadership effectiveness" (p. 173).

Researchers cite additional examples of role modeling by principals of high-achieving schools. In his analysis of the relationship between school culture and achievement, Stolp concludes that

> the most effective change in school culture happens when principals, teachers, and students model the values and beliefs important to the institution. The actions of the principal are noticed and interpreted by others as 'what is important.' (p. 4)

Black's review also concerns the relationship of culture to achievement (plus belongingness and motivation) and concludes that "culture-shaping principals . . . set a consistent example of core values in daily routines" (p. 33). Study of successful principals led Gersten and Carnine (1981) to conclude that "the administrator should serve as a model of commitment to the school improvement plan" (quoted in Walberg & Lane, 1985, p. 228).

On her experience in turning a low-performing school into a high-performing one, Butler comments, "I modeled what I valued, and I invested my time the way I wanted [the teachers] to invest theirs" (p. 31). Coyle and Witcher's (1992) summary found that the effective principal serves as a "role model for students and staff alike" (p. 391). In their analysis of the kinds of power and authority effective principals exercise, High and Achilles comment on their "norm-setting power—the principal models desired behaviors, e.g., 'This is the way we treat kids at this school'" (p. 9). High and Achilles go on to say that

> prospective principals should be involved in simulations of specific norm-setting behaviors so they can learn to model to their future teaching co-workers a commitment to school goals and a non-manipulative approach to leadership. (p. 20)

It may be that the single most important thing that principals model is love for the children in their schools. Gantner (1997) and Gantner and colleagues (1999) found, not surprisingly, that this is what parents care about most in a school principal. Scheurich's summary of the operating principles of successful school administrators includes the admonition that "all children must be treated with love, appreciation, care, and respect—no exceptions allowed." Finally, Cash, who was National Distinguished Principal in 1997, speaks to the importance of role modeling—and love:

> I can teach someone how to teach. I can model effective instructional strategies and individualize a plan of action that helps a teacher acquire the necessary skills to be successful. What I can't do is perform a heart transplant to give a person that genuine love for children. (1997, p. 24)

What These Principals *Don't* Do

It might be worthwhile to look briefly at what principals of high-performing schools *do not do*. Much of this can, of course, be extrapolated from what we have learned they do in fact do. But some researchers have called specific attention to approaches the effective principals avoid. Bartell, after noting that the outstanding principals in her study "do what they can and must do in order to support, facilitate, encourage, motivate, recognize, and reward good teaching," goes on to say that "absent from [the principals'] responses were such verbs as control, manage, direct, command, and regulate" (p. 121).

Firestone and Wilson found that tight administrative control over teaching is negatively related to student achievement (p. 27), and Bista and Glasman (1997) report the same finding. Gaziel's administrative time-use study reveals that, whereas principals of high-performing schools expend generous amounts of time "in instructional leadership activities, student relationships, teachers' professional development, and parent-principal contact," average principals "spend nearly all of their time on organizational maintenance and pupil control activities" (1995, pp. 179–180).

Endnotes

1. The list of research support for each component is long and potentially distracting for the reader. Thus, I have identified the supporting articles in footnotes, avoiding citations in text except when material is directly quoted. The research support for these assertions is from Bartell, 1990; Black, 1997; Chase & Kane, 1983; Cotton, 2000; Edmonds, 1979; Glasman, 1984; Heck, Larsen & Marcoulides, 1990; Heck & Marcoulides, 1993; Hipp, 1996; Larsen, 1987; Leitner, 1994; Sammons, Hillman & Mortimore, 1995; and Scheurich, 1998.

2. See Bartell, 1990; Bates, 1993; Black, 1997; Chase & Kane, 1983; Cheng, 1994; Cotton, 2000; Coyle & Witcher, 1992; Gurr, 1997; Hallinger, Bickman & Davis, 1996; Heck, Larsen & Marcoulides, 1990; Heck & Marcoulides, 1993; Johnson & Asera, 1999; Kirby, Paradise & King, 1992; Krug, 1992; Larsen, 1987; Manasse, 1984; Mendez-Morse, 1991; Peterson, Gok & Warren, 1995; Renchler, 1992; Sagor, 1992; Sammons, Hillman & Mortimore, 1995; Scheurich, 1998; Short & Spencer, 1990; Silins, 1994; Sizemore, 1985; Valentine & Bowman, 1991; and Wendel, Hoke, & Joekel, 1996.

3. Referenced in Bartell, 1990; Bates, 1993; Binkowski, Cordeiro & Iwanicki, 1995; Butler, 1997; Chase & Kane, 1983; Cheng, 1994; Davis,

1998; Evans & Teddlie, 1995; Gantner, 1997; Gullatt & Lofton, 1996; Heck, Larsen & Marcoulides, 1990; Heck & Marcoulides, 1993; Johnson & Asera, 1999; Kirby, Paradise & King, 1992; Larsen, 1987; Reavis, Vinson & Fox, 1999; Sammons et al., 1998; Scheurich, 1998; Short & Spencer, 1990; Sizemore, 1985; Steller, 1988; Valentine & Bowman, 1991; Wendel, Hoke & Joekel, 1996; and Zigarelli, 1996.

4. See Chase & Kane, 1983; Davis, 1998; Johnson & Asera, 1999; Scarnati, 1994; Wagstaff et al., 1998; and Wendel, Hoke & Joekel, 1996.

5. Consult Bamburg & Andrews, 1991; Bartell, 1990; Black, 1997; Gantner, 1997; McCallum, 1999; Reavis, Vinson & Fox, 1999; and Short & Spencer, 1990.

6. Found in Bartell, 1990; Black, 1997; Bulach, Lunenburg & McCallon, 1994; Davis, 1998; Gullatt & Lofton, 1996; Hallinger, Bickman & Davis, 1996; Hipp, 1996; Johnson & Asera, 1999; Johnson & Holdaway, 1991; Larsen, 1987; Short & Spencer, 1990; Silins, 1994; Steller, 1988; and Thomas, 1997.

7. See Binkowski, Cordeiro & Iwanicki, 1995; Black, 1997; Charles & Karr-Kidwell, 1995; Davis, 1998; Gantner et al., 1999; Gaziel, 1995; Gullatt & Lofton, 1996; Sammons et al., 1998; Stolp, 1991; and Wendel, Hoke, & Joekel, 1996.

8. See, for example, Bates, 1993; Davis, 1998; DeBevoise, 1984; Evans & Teddlie, 1995; Hipp, 1996; Scarnati, 1994; Thomas, 1997; Valentine & Bowman, 1991; and Wendel, Hoke & Joekel, 1996.

9. See Bartell, 1990; Black, 1997; Bulach, Lunenburg & McCallon, 1994; Cotton, 1992; Davis, 1998; Gaziel, 1995; Heck, Larsen & Marcoulides, 1990; Heck & Marcoulides, 1993; High & Achilles, 1986; Johnson & Asera, 1999; Johnson & Holdaway, 1991; Leithwood & Montgomery, 1982; Sammons, Hillman & Mortimore, 1995; Scheurich, 1998; Sizemore, 1985; Steller, 1988; and Teddlie & Reynolds, 2000.

10. See Bartell, 1990; Binkowski, Cordeiro & Iwanicki, 1995; Blase & Blase, 1994; Cotton, 1992; Davis, 1998; DeBevoise, 1984; Delaney, 1997; Gaziel, 1995; Gullatt & Lofton, 1996; Heck, 1993; Heck, Larsen & Marcoulides, 1990; Heck & Marcoulides, 1993; High & Achilles, 1986; Hipp, 1996; Johnson & Asera, 1999; Leithwood & Montgomery, 1982; Peterson, Gok & Warren, 1995; and Teddlie & Reynolds, 2000.

11. Outlined in Bartell, 1990; Evans & Teddlie, 1995; Gullatt & Lofton, 1996; Heck, 1993; Hipp, 1996; Johnson & Asera, 1999; Leithwood & Montgomery, 1982; McCallum, 1999; Peterson, Gok & Warren, 1995; Riordan & da Costa, 1998; Scheurich, 1998; Stolp, 1991; Thomas, 1997; and Valentine & Bowman, 1991.

12. For findings about instructional leadership in general, see Bartell, 1990; Coyle & Witcher, 1992; Gaziel, 1995; Gullatt & Lofton, 1996; Krug, 1992; Mendez-Morse, 1991; Pavan & Reid, 1994; Steller, 1988; and Walberg & Lane, 1985.

13. For research support see Black, 1997; Butler, 1997; Davis, 1998; DeBevoise, 1984; Gaziel, 1995; Glasman, 1984; Johnson & Asera, 1999; Kirby, Paradise & King, 1992; Leithwood & Montgomery, 1982; Manasse, 1984; Peterson, Gok & Warren, 1995; Reavis, Vinson & Fox, 1999; Renchler, 1992; Sagor, 1992; Sammons, Hillman & Mortimore, 1995; Sammons et al., 1998; Scheurich, 1998; Silins, 1994; Sizemore, 1985; Steller, 1998; and Wendel, Hoke & Joekel, 1996.

14. See especially Bartell, 1990; Chase & Kane, 1983; DeBevoise, 1984; Leithwood & Montgomery, 1982; McCallum, 1999; Sagor, 1992; and Scheurich, 1998.

15. Bamburg & Andrews, 1991; Binkowski, Cordeiro & Iwanicki, 1995; Heck, 1992; Heck, Larsen & Marcoulides, 1990; Heck & Marcoulides, 1993; High & Achilles, 1986; Johnson & Asera, 1999;

Larsen, 1987; Sagor, 1992; Sammons, Hillman & Mortimore, 1995; and Walberg & Lane, 1985.

16. See Butler, 1997; DeBevoise, 1984; Evans & Teddlie, 1995; Heck, 1992; Heck, Larsen & Marcoulides, 1990; Larsen, 1987; Leitner, 1994; McCallum, 1999; Mendez-Morse, 1991; Sagor, 1992; Short & Spencer, 1990; Sizemore, 1985; and Walberg & Lane, 1985.

17. Researchers addressing this issue include Gullatt & Lofton, 1996; Heck, 1993; Heck, Larsen & Marcoulides, 1990; and Heck & Marcoulides, 1993.

18. Butler, 1997; Hipp, 1996; Reitzug, 1997; Sagor, 1992; Scheurich, 1998; and Wendel, Hoke & Joekel, 1996.

19. Bartell, 1990; Binkowski, Cordeiro & Iwanicki, 1995; Butler, 1997; Cheng, 1994; Cotton, 1992; Gaziel, 1995; Johnson & Asera, 1999; Kirby, Paradise & King, 1992; Leithwood & Montgomery, 1982; Leitner, 1994; Levine & Levine, 2000; Mendez-Morse, 1991; Peterson, Gok & Warren, 1995; Sammons, Hillman & Mortimore, 1995; and Wagstaff et al., 1998.

20. Bamburg & Andrews, 1991; Chase & Kane, 1983; DeBevoise, 1984; Edmonds, 1979; Evans & Teddlie, 1995; Gurr, 1997; Heck, Larsen & Marcoulides, 1990; Heck & Marcoulides, 1993; Johnson & Asera, 1999; Larsen, 1987; Leithwood & Montgomery, 1982; Mendez-Morse, 1991; and Short & Spencer, 1990.

21. Bartell, 1990; Black, 1997; Cotton, 2000; Evans & Teddlie, 1995; and Johnson & Asera, 1999.

22. Bartell, 1990; DeBevoise, 1984; Gullatt & Lofton, 1996; Heck, Larsen & Marcoulides, 1990; Krug, 1992; Larsen, 1987; McCallum, 1999; Sammons, Hillman & Mortimore, 1995; Sizemore, 1985; Steller, 1988; Teddlie & Reynolds, 2000; Wagstaff et al., 1998; and Walberg & Lane, 1985.

23. See Bartell, 1990; Butler, 1997; Glasman, 1984; Gullatt & Lofton, 1996; Heck, 1992; Johnson & Asera, 1999; Levine & Levine, 2000; and Mendez-Morse, 1991.

24. Supporting research includes Bartell, 1990; Heck, Larsen & Marcoulides, 1990; Heck & Marcoulides, 1993; High & Achilles, 1986; Hipp, 1996; Johnson & Holdaway, 1991; Reavis, Vinson & Fox, 1999; Scarnati, 1994; Short & Spencer, 1990; Walberg & Lane, 1985; and Wendel, Hoke & Joekel, 1996.

25. Bamburg & Andrews, 1991; Black, 1997; Butler, 1997; Coyle & Witcher, 1992; High & Achilles, 1986; Hipp, 1996; Kirby, Paradise & King, 1992; Stolp, 1991; Wagstaff et al., 1998; and Walberg & Lane, 1985.

2

OTHER KEY RESEARCH FINDINGS ABOUT PRINCIPALS

The Leadership of Male and Female Principals

SOME RESEARCHERS HAVE INVESTIGATED THE DIFFERENCES BETWEEN the approaches to leadership taken by male and female principals and the results of those differences.[1] Pavan and Reid (1994) find that the tendencies linked to success are more commonly found in female principals than in their male counterparts—especially instructional leadership and the establishment of supportive climates. Ortiz and Marshall's extensive 1988 summary of gender comparison studies reports that female principals contribute to higher teacher performance and student achievement because they are more actively involved with instructional leadership activities and spend more time on supervision and other instructional tasks (pp. 134–135).

In a similar vein, Bulach, Boothe, and Michael's 1999 study of trust/decision making, control, instructional leadership, human relations, and conflict finds that female principals received significantly higher instructional leadership ratings than male principals did.

Initially, the researchers were surprised by the finding that "female principals are much better than male principals in instructional leadership" (p. 9). Upon closer examination, however, they offered what may be at least a partial explanation of the finding. Georgia, where the research took place, has a leadership certification procedure that allows high school teachers with an administrative certificate to become elementary principals. As it happens, many of the male elementary principals in the study were high school trained, while most of the female elementary principals were elementary trained. "It would follow that elementary trained principals would be able to provide better instructional leadership than an elementary principal who had a secondary background" (p. 9).

A meta-analysis conducted by Eagly, Karau, and Johnson (1992) found that women principals tend to lead in a more democratic, participative manner than their male counterparts. The researchers write that this finding suggests that women who occupy the principal role are more likely than men to treat teachers and other organizational subordinates as colleagues and equals and to invite participation in decision making. Men evidently adopt a less collaborative style and are relatively more dominating and directive than women. (p. 91)

Shakeshaft (1989) finds that, compared with male principals, female principals

1. Are more person oriented, have better interpersonal skills, and create school environments that are more person oriented and more encouraging of community involvement (p. 174).

2. Are better informed about pedagogy, more inclined to be direct instructional leaders, and create climates that are more conducive to learning (pp. 173–174).

3. Adopt a more democratic, participatory leadership style, and encourage and develop a stronger sense of school community and one where achievement is emphasized (p. 187).

Shakeshaft's explanations for the differences she found are as follows:

1. Differential ability in the males and females aspiring to a teaching career. This is due to past differences in the available career choices for women and men; thus, women who became teachers were of higher ability than men (p. 169).

2. Differences in motivation, with more women likely to want to be teachers than men (pp. 70–71).

3. Differences in experience, with women taking longer to become school administrators (p. 63).

4. Differences in communication patterns including supervisory conferences, critical feedback, and interpretation (p. 181).

Hallinger, Bickman, and Davis's 1996 study focuses chiefly on the means by which principals' leadership affects student achievement, but it also finds that "female principals exercised more active leadership in the areas of curriculum and instruction than males" (p. 543).

Bista and Glasman's study did not directly address the matter of gender and leadership, but it did find that the more teaching experience a principal has had, the more flexible his or her leadership style is likely to be. Since women tend to have spent more time as teachers before becoming principals than men have, and since flexibility is identified as a positive principal characteristic, this research suggests that female principals may have an advantage as school leaders.

Finally, following his examination of the research on male versus female principals, Gurr writes,

> the leadership required for schools now and in the future seems more attuned to the type of leadership that has been found to be more typical of females than males. This may result in the marginalization of male principals,

but more likely will enrich schools through the liberation of leadership roles from a more constrained, non-inclusive perspective. (p. 14)

Elementary and Secondary Principals

Bartell's survey and interviews of outstanding secondary principals produced a list of instructional leadership behaviors virtually identical to those identified in this report for principals in general. For example, the secondary principals identified their top four areas of responsibility as (1) evaluating teacher performance, (2) providing a supportive climate, (3) articulating the goals of the school, and (4) providing an orderly atmosphere for learning. They also cite team orientation, shared leadership, and encouragement of professional growth as some of the other attributes of effective principals.

No doubt many secondary principals would give similar responses. However, as Heck discovered in his 1992 analysis of principals' time expenditures, secondary principals, as a group, spend substantially less time on key instructional tasks than do elementary principals. In particular, they spend less time observing classroom practices, promoting discussion about instructional issues, and emphasizing the use of test results for program improvement (p. 30).[2]

Some researchers have suggested that secondary principals might be less involved with certain functions because of subject matter specialization at the secondary level. As Teddlie and Reynolds (2000) quite reasonably point out, "it is probably impossible for a secondary principal to be an expert in all instructional areas covered by a secondary curriculum; thus, this instructional leadership role will be shared with the department chairs" (p. 180). Alternatively, Riordan and da Costa's work suggests that principals' efforts to encourage collaboration might be more fruitful if they developed ways for teachers of the same subject *in different schools* to meet and collaborate (p. 10).

Principals in High- and Low-SES Schools

Researchers tell us that principals in schools with substantial numbers of poor children are less likely to be instructional leaders than are principals in middle class or affluent schools.[3] Leitner (1994) finds that principals in schools with a high SES were not only more likely to manage instruction than their counterparts in low-SES schools, but that they were also less directive and more collaborative (pp. 233–234). Mendez-Morse's summary distinguishes between "managers," who oversee operations and maintain the status quo, and "leaders," who foster and direct change toward a vision for improvement of the organization. She finds that low-SES schools are much more likely to have managers at the helm than leaders.

Firestone and Wilson's analysis, which differentiates between principals who primarily exercise control over teachers and those who chiefly provide support for them, finds the former to be much more prevalent in lower-SES schools (p. 22).

Meanwhile, research points to the instructional leadership of the principal as the key element in the success of those low-SES schools where student achievement is higher than their demographic profile would predict. In transforming a low-performing, low-SES, inner-city school into a high-performing one, Butler credits the cluster of instructional leadership behaviors described at length in this paper—particularly setting ambitious goals, communicating high expectations of students and teachers, using student performance data to plan instruction, maintaining a focus on raising student achievement, and supporting teachers' professional development and experimentation.

Mendez-Morse's 1991 analysis produced the same finding. As she puts it,

> Principals in schools where at-risk students are achieving practice the skills and apply the knowledge of effective instructional leadership. They have a vision—a picture of what they want students to achieve. They engage teachers, parents, students and others to share in creating the vision. They encourage them to join in the efforts to make that vision a reality. They keep the vision in the forefront by supporting teachers' instructional efforts and by guiding the use of data to evaluate the progress of the school. (p. 2)

Evans and Teddlie find that the leadership style of "initiator" is most effective in raising achievement in low-SES schools. Not surprisingly, the profile of the principal as initiator encompasses the vigorous instructional leadership behaviors found to benefit the achievement of students in general. In the Texas African-American Research Project of Wagstaff and colleagues, the three districts whose low-SES students exhibited high achievement were characterized by this kind of principal support and leadership.

This point may have been made most forcefully by Scheurich, whose project was undertaken to find out why low-SES children of color achieved so well in certain school environments. As we have seen repeatedly in this examination, the principal's leadership was found to be at the heart of the schools' success.

Principals' Impact on Student Outcomes

As noted at the beginning of this examination, much of the early research on the impact of principals on student outcomes began and ended with the finding that a relationship exists. Hallinger and Heck (1996) write that

> Although at the hortatory level there is little disagreement concerning the belief that principals have an impact on the lives of teachers and students, both the nature and degree of that effect continues to be open to debate. . . . This relationship is complex and not easily subject to

■

> empirical verification. . . . Unfortunately, as prior review-
> ers of this literature have concluded, the tradition of
> principal-effectiveness studies has not generally done
> justice to this complexity. (p. 6)

It was left to subsequent researchers to look into the matter of *how* the effects on students occur.[4] In general, these researchers find that, while a small portion of the effect may be direct—that is, principals' direct interactions with students in or out of the classroom may be motivating, inspiring, instructive, or otherwise influential—most of it is indirect, that is, mediated through teachers and others. For example, Hallinger, Bickman, and Davis's analysis finds

> a strong relation between the degree of instructional
> leadership provided by the principal and the existence of
> a clear school mission. A clear mission, in turn, influ-
> enced student opportunity to learn and teachers' expec-
> tations for student achievement. This constellation of
> instructional climate variables had a positive subsequent
> effect on student achievement in reading. (p. 543)

Leitner, too, finds that principals' effects on student achievement are indirect and complex, being mediated through principal-teacher interactions. He notes that principals in high-achieving schools use more of what he calls "cultural linkages," primarily the norms and values regarding successful instruction and student learning (p. 224). Jean Russell (1997) writes that school leadership influences student progress by an indirect process, through its influence on teachers. The crucial leadership characteristic in this process was found to be leadership support—leadership that is reliable, approachable, supportive, engaging in good communication and aware of problems faced by teachers. (quoted in Gurr, 1997, p. 8)

Hallinger and Heck's work posits a similar model of the way principals' behaviors affect student achievement indirectly—one that traces their actions through school policies and norms to the practices of teachers and on to the students.

Lest readers form the impression that "indirect effect" means less effect or less important effect, Hallinger and Heck explicitly counsel against such a view:

The fact that leadership effects on school achievement appear to be indirect is neither cause for alarm or dismay. As noted previously, achieving results through others is the essence of leadership. A finding that principal effects are mediated by other in-school variables does nothing whatsoever to diminish the principal's importance. (p. 39)

Transactional and Transformational Leadership

Theorists have written extensively about "transactional" and "transformational" leadership on the part of school principals and discussed the relative merits of these approaches. And researchers, for their part, have compared the leadership approaches that go by these names.[5] Since the examination of theory is outside the scope of this paper, suffice it to say that "transactional" refers to a type of leadership in which the principal has a bureaucratic orientation and seeks ways to appeal to the self-interest of staff members as a strategy for inducing them to carry out his or her bidding.

Transformational leadership works by "tapping the shared values of followers and building normative commitment to the mission of the school" (Peterson and Lezotte, 1991, quoted in Gurr, 1997, p. 4). As such, it is concerned with influencing staff members to transcend their self-interest and focus on the best interests of their students. Thomas goes so far as to say that "the transformational leader is one who motivates followers to perform above expectations" (p. 8). Silins (1992) distinguishes the two approaches as follows:

> Transactional leadership relies on an exchange relationship between leader and followers, while transformational leadership sets aside the self-centered interests of the followers to bring about enhanced performance and change. (pp. 328–329)

Leithwood and Jantzi (1999) point out that "current educational leadership literature offers no unitary concept of transformational leadership" (p. 453), and theorists truly offer somewhat different views. Some, for example, note that transformational leaders both incorporate transactional leadership approaches and move beyond them. The important thing is that the elements of these various conceptions mirror the behavior of principals in high-performing schools: establishing a worthy vision and clear goals, providing individualized support to staff, holding high performance expectations, engaging others in decision making, and so on. Not surprisingly, researchers find that transformational leadership is positively related to student achievement and is more effective than the deal-making between principal and staff that characterizes the transactional approach alone.

Effects on Principals' Leadership

So far this discussion has focused on the effects *of* principals' leadership. But some of the researchers also looked at the effects of various factors *on* principals' leadership.[6] This line of research concerns itself with factors that can enhance or constrain principals' pursuit of their goals.

Hallinger, Bickman, and Davis find that high levels of parent involvement have a positive effect on principal effectiveness, as does working in higher-SES schools (pp. 540–541). Being female, as previously noted, is positively related to instructional leadership (p. 543). Heck's analysis indicates that new principals in low-achieving schools frequently encounter considerable resistance to their ideas and are thus constrained in their effectiveness (p. 31). Leitner, too, notes that principals have limitations on their ability to be effective—limitations imposed by the willingness of teachers, students, and parents to cooperate and collaborate with them (p. 236).

This research does not overturn the many findings about principals' influence on schooling practices and student outcomes. Instead, it serves as a caution against a simplistic belief that a principal singlehandedly makes the school what it is. "The problems of reforming low-achieving schools may extend beyond merely changing principals," writes Heck (1992), "and it may be too much to assume that one person can reshape these schools in a lasting manner" (p. 31).

The Dearth of Instructional Leadership

Scores of studies show that student achievement is strongly affected by the leadership of school principals. Principals who serve as instructional leaders, in particular, are much more likely to have high-achieving students than principals who do not. So it is discouraging to find, as the researchers have, that principals who do function as instructional leaders are relatively rare.[7] After reviewing research on the benefits of principals who function this way, Walberg and Lane conclude their 1985 summary with a disheartening observation: "The reality is that in most schools, the principal is not an instructional leader" (p. 272). Steller's review leads him to make the same call: "There is currently a shortage of instructional leaders in the principalship" (p. 16).

Other researchers elaborate on this widespread lack of leadership. Following his 1992 study, Heck writes that, "as previous research has indicated . . . typical principals ignore the instructional planning strategies of teachers in all but exceptional circumstances" (p. 30). He notes that conditions at schools with a history of low performance might be partly to blame. "New leaders in organizations may encounter problems with trying to change existing norms of behavior. . . . Instead they tend to adjust to the existing norms" (p. 31). Hence, new principals in low-performing schools are more likely to adapt to the norms that have been keeping the school's performance low than to bring about change— or even try to do so.

Manasse cites research indicating that effective principals more closely resemble leaders of high-performing organizations than they do ordinary principals. Whereas the latter are relatively reactive and disinclined to press for change, the former are proactive, pushing the organization to achieve their vision; applying the analytical and interpersonal skills to move others toward the organization's goals; and using symbols, slogans, and so on to inspire staff and constituents.

Apparently, the majority of principals who do not spend their time being instructional leaders are instead either drowning in the "sea of administrivia" referred to by Leithwood and Montgomery or dealing with student behavior issues. Gaziel's time-use study leads him to observe that although the literature is clear about what principals should do to become effective (high performing), studies of actual time utilization by principals typically indicate that principals do not act in such a fashion. This research shows that principals spend nearly all of their time on organizational maintenance and pupil control activities. (p. 180)

Developing and Improving Principals' Leadership

Gaziel goes on to say that, in order for more schools to become high performing

principals must plan their time to enable them to spend most of it in instructional leadership activities, student relationships, teachers' professional development, and parent-principal contact, whereas management should be de-emphasized. (pp. 179–180)

And indeed, many leadership development programs for principals are now available to help veteran, new, and aspiring principals acquire the knowledge and skills needed to foster improved student performance. Whether these programs will be successful remains to be seen, and will depend in part on how transferable leadership expertise proves to be. As Cash observed in 1997, if principals lack the foundational love for children that seems a key element of effectiveness, we cannot give them a "heart transplant" and instill them with it. And Scarnati identifies a whole range of admirable character traits that principals should possess, in addition to "technical competence" (p. 76).

Kirby, Paradise, and King's 1992 research studies provide reasons for optimism, however. They find that, although qualities of personality such as "charisma" may play a role in leadership effectiveness, more important still are "observable, *teachable* leader behaviors such as intellectual stimulation" (p. 310). They go on to say that

> our finding has direct implications for the training of future leaders in education. It refutes the 'leaders are born, not made' adage, suggesting that skills in educating and challenging followers should be major considerations in leadership training. (p. 310)

Endnotes

1. See Bulach, Boothe, & Michael, 1999; Eagly, Karau, & Johnson, 1992; Gurr, 1997; Hallinger, Bickman, & Davis, 1996; Ortiz & Marshall, 1988; Pavan & Reid, 1994; and Shakeshaft, 1989.

2. See Bartell, 1990; Heck, 1992; and Riordan & da Costa, 1998.

3. Researchers who have compared principals' behaviors in high- and low-SES schools include Butler, 1997; Evans & Teddlie, 1995; Firestone & Wilson, 1989; Leitner, 1994; Mendez-Morse, 1991; Scheurich, 1998; and Wagstaff et al., 1998.

4. Researchers who have looked into how the effect of principals on students occurs include Gurr, 1997; Hallinger, Bickman & Davis, 1996; Hallinger & Heck, 1996; and Leitner, 1994.

5. See Gurr, 1997; Johnson & Asera, 1999; Leithwood & Jantzi, 1999; Silins, 1992; and Thomas, 1997.

6. See Hallinger, Bickman, & Davis, 1996; Heck, 1992; and Leitner, 1994.

7. See Gaziel, 1995; Heck, 1992; Leithwood & Montgomery, 1982; Manasse, 1984; Steller, 1988; and Walberg & Lane, 1985.

SUMMARY

Key points made in this analysis are as follows:

1. Research from the 1970s and early 1980s shows that strong administrative leadership, including instructional leadership, is a key component of schools with high student achievement.

2. More recent research has confirmed and expanded the findings of the earlier research.

3. The research base on the effects of principals' leadership on students is large and varied. It includes different kinds of research designs, focuses on different subject groups, and is concerned with both academic and affective student outcomes. A substantial portion of the research focuses on poor, largely minority student populations.

4. Many leadership behaviors and traits of principals are positively related to student achievement, attitudes, and social behavior. Principals of high-achieving schools are effective in the following areas:

   a. Safe and orderly school environment. Effective principals involve others, including students, in setting standards for student behavior. They communicate high expectations for behavior, and they apply rules consistently from day to day and from student to student. They expect teachers to handle most disciplinary matters, and they provide in-school suspension with support for seriously disruptive students. They foster a sense of responsibility in students for appropriate behavior and work to create an environment that encourages such behavior.

b. Vision and goals focused on high levels of student learning. Effective principals work with others to establish a vision of the ideal school and clear goals related to the vision. They continually emphasize the academic goals of the school and the importance of learning.

c. High expectations for student achievement. Successful principals expect, and encourage their staffs to expect, all students to reach their learning potential. They ensure that students understand that school personnel believe in their abilities.

d. Self-confidence, responsibility, and perseverance. Principals of high-achieving schools see themselves as responsible for their schools' success and believe they can successfully work through others to achieve it. They continue to pursue their goals despite difficulties and setbacks.

e. Visibility and accessibility. Successful principals make themselves available to teachers, students, and others in the school community. They frequently visit classrooms to observe and interact with teachers and students.

f. Positive and supportive school climate. This is closely related to the principal's efforts to maintain safety and good order, and includes such elements as encouraging schoolwide communication of interest and caring to students. Almost everything that the principal says and does contributes to the overall school climate.

g. Communication and interaction. Effective principals are good communicators who share with and solicit information from all groups in the school community. They thereby build positive relationships that enhance all school functions.

h. Emotional/interpersonal support. These principals are capable and caring communicators in the interpersonal realm who are aware and supportive of the personal needs of staff and students.

i. Parent/community outreach and involvement. Principals of successful schools conduct vigorous outreach to parents and community members, including those who are traditionally underrepresented in parent involvement programs. They seek and support parent/community involvement in both instruction and governance.

j. Rituals, ceremonies, and other symbolic actions. Effective principals make use of school rituals and ceremonies to honor tradition, instill pride, recognize excellence, and strengthen a sense of affiliation with the school on the part of all those connected to it.

k. Shared leadership/decision making and staff empowerment. The most successful principals engage their staffs and constituents in participative decision making. They ensure that everyone involved has the information and training needed to make this process productive.

l. Collaboration. Closely related to shared leadership are the collaborative practices of principals in high-achieving schools. These principals establish an environment in which they and their staffs learn, plan, and work together to improve their schools.

m. The importance of instructional leadership. A key difference between highly effective and less effective principals is that the former are actively involved in the curricular and instructional life of their schools.

n. High levels of student learning. Principals of high-achieving schools have a sustained focus on promoting student achievement. They make decisions in light of the potential impact on student learning and work to engage others in efforts to foster high student performance.

o. Norm of continuous improvement. Recognizing that "you don't have to be bad to get better," principals of high-performing schools continually push for improvement. They ensure that this process is a permanent part of school life.

p. Discussion of instructional issues. Successful principals facilitate discussion among staff about curriculum and instruction, and engage in these discussions themselves.

q. Classroom observation and feedback to teachers. Effective principals frequently visit classrooms, observing instruction and providing feedback to teachers in the spirit of coaching as well as evaluation.

r. Teacher autonomy. Principals of effective schools respect their teachers' skills and judgment, and allow them considerable autonomy in organizing and managing their classrooms. They also protect staff from excessive intrusion by forces outside the school.

s. Support of risk taking. Effective principals take calculated risks to improve their schools and encourage teachers to do the same by being innovative and experimenting in the classroom.

t. Professional development opportunities and resources. Principals of high-achieving schools offer more, and more varied, professional development activities than those in lower achieving schools. They are creative in securing the resources—financial, human, time, materials, and facilities —the school needs to improve.

u. Instructional time. Principals of successful schools protect instructional time by keeping loudspeaker announcements, other administrative intrusions, and noninstructional activities from taking too much of the school day. They arrange for additional learning time during and beyond the school day as needed.

v. Monitoring student progress and sharing findings. Successful principals ensure that there are systematic procedures for monitoring student progress at both schoolwide and classroom levels. They also ensure that data are disaggregated to monitor the progress of specific groups. They communicate findings to everyone in the school community.

w. Use of student data for program improvement. Effective principals know how to interpret student performance data and use it in planning for curricular and instructional improvement.

x. Recognition of student and staff achievement. Successful principals make a point of recognizing achievement and improvement on the part of both students and staff.

y. Role modeling. Effective principals "walk their talk," exemplifying the outlook and behavior they expect from staff and students. They do this by working with staff in professional development activities; apportioning their own time in ways that support student learning; and treating students, staff, and constituents with respect.

z. What principals don't do. Effective principals avoid imposing tight administrative control over others in the school. Their description of their work is notable for its exclusion of terms such as "manage, direct, command, and regulate." They do not allow desk work to take over their lives, nor do they allow their disciplinary activities to outweigh their supportive ones.

5. Researchers report many other findings about principals in addition to their effects on student outcomes. They include:

a. The leadership of male and female principals. Effective leadership behaviors—and instructional leadership and the establishment of positive climates—are more frequently observed in female principals than in male principals, possibly due to the different routes they typically take to become principals.

b. Elementary and secondary principals. Elementary principals are more likely to assume instructional leadership responsibilities than secondary principals are. This may be partly due to the subject-matter specialization in secondary schools.

c. Principals in high- and low-SES schools. Principals in low-SES schools are less likely to be instructional leaders than those in higher-SES schools. They are also less collaborative and more directive.

d. How principals affect student outcomes. Principals' behaviors have little direct impact on student outcomes but substantial indirect impact—that is, impact mediated through teachers and others.

e. Transactional and transformational leadership. Transactional leadership, in which principals appeal to staff members' self-interest to induce staff to do their bidding, is less effective than transformational leadership, which inspires staff to transcend their self-interest and focus on the best interests of students.

f. Effects on *principals' leadership.* The type of leadership exercised by the principal is influenced by numerous factors, the most important of which are the achievement history and norms of the school.

g. The dearth of instructional leadership. Most principals are not instructional leaders, being primarily engaged instead by administrative and disciplinary activities. Some research indicates, however, that the requisite behaviors are observable and teachable.

Conclusion

Can the importance of the principal's role in fostering student achievement be overstated? The principal does not affect student performance single-handedly, of course, or even directly. Yet the evidence clearly shows that, working with others in the ways outlined in this report, principals do have a profound and positive influence on student learning. The converse is also true: High-achieving schools whose principals do not lead in these ways are difficult to find. So difficult, in fact, that veteran researcher Lawrence Lezotte has gone so far as to say, "If you know of an effective school without an effective principal, call me collect."

KATHLEEN COTTON DIED ON JULY 5, 2002, AT AGE 56—MUCH TOO soon. Most people knew Kathleen for the research synthesis work she did for nearly 20 years at the Northwest Regional Educational Laboratory. She pioneered and perfected a non-technical approach to synthesizing large bodies of research and putting the supportable findings into clear, concise language that busy educators could read and understand quickly. Kathleen produced reviews on many, many topics, ranging from smaller learning communities to class size.

Kathleen distinguished herself by producing consistently high-quality work over many years. She was

- The most published Northwest Lab staff member ever,
- Author of the most widely distributed and used Northwest Lab publication, *Effective Schooling Practices: A Research Synthesis,* now published by ASCD under the title, *Research You Can Use to Improve Results,*
- The most quoted staff member ever at Northwest Lab,
- Primary author and editor of the School Improvement Research Series, one of the most frequently accessed sections of the Northwest Lab Web page.

Kathleen Cotton was the first recipient of the Jerry Kirkpatrick Distinguished Service Award in June 2002, a well-deserved recognition of the major contributions she made to the Northwest Regional Educational Laboratory and the field of education.

ANNOTATED REFERENCES

Bamburg, J. E., & Andrews, R. L. (1991). School goals, principals, and achievement. *School Effectiveness and School Improvement, 2*(3), 175–191.

Compares 10 high-achieving and 10 low-achieving elementary schools in terms of goal orientation and instructional leadership behaviors on the part of the principal. High-achieving schools place greater emphasis on academic excellence than their low-achieving counterparts, and their principals emphasize and engage in instruction-related activities to a greater degree.

Bartell, C. A. (1990). Outstanding secondary principals reflect on instructional leadership. *The High School Journal, 73*(2), 118–128.

Reports on a study in which "outstanding principals of the year" described their instructional leadership beliefs and behaviors. Among numerous findings were that they identified their top four areas of responsibility as (1) evaluating teacher performance, (2) providing a supportive climate, (3) articulating the goals of the school, and (4) providing an orderly atmosphere for learning. All their activities were geared toward promoting effective teaching and learning.

Bates, J. T. (1993, Spring). Portrait of a successful rural alternative school. *The Rural Educator, 14*(3), 20–24.

Describes the results of a case study of a small, rural alternative school where student learning outcomes are very positive despite numerous risk factors. The author/researcher identified several factors responsible for the school's success, including the principal's instructional leadership and support of the staff.

Binkowski, K., Cordeiro, P., & Iwanicki, E. (1995, April). *A qualitative study of higher and lower performing elementary schools*. Paper presented at the annual meeting of the American Educational Research Association, San Francisco. (ERIC Document Reproduction Service No. ED386311)

Gives an account of a study of two high-performing and two low-performing elementary schools to identify differences in leadership, school culture, and instructional factors. The authors find that, in contrast to the low-performing schools, the high-performing schools had administrators who involved all staff in goal setting, facilitated internal and external communication through both formal and informal means, and provided more professional development opportunities.

Bista, M. B., & Glasman, N. S. (1997). Principals' approaches to leadership, their antecedents and student outcomes. *Journal of School Leadership, 8,* 109–136.

Uses data on California school principals to determine relationships among four approaches to leadership, other principal characteristics, and student achievement. The authors found that a political, power-oriented approach correlates positively with student achievement; the more teaching experience a principal has, the more flexible his or her leadership style; populations that are predominantly poor or nonwhite have the lowest academic performance; and the larger the school, the more likely the principal is to use a political approach to leadership.

Black, S. (1997, June). Creating community. *American School Board Journal, 184*(6), 32–35.

Reviews recent research on the nature of school culture and climate and identifies behaviors on the part of the principal that have been shown to enhance culture and climate and thereby improve student belongingness, motivation, and achievement.

Blase, J., & Blase, J. R. (1994). *Empowering teachers: What successful principals do.* Thousand Oaks, CA: Corwin Press.

Identifies the nature of teacher empowerment and, based on a study in which teachers described what their principals do to empower them, provides guidelines for other principals to use. Principal behaviors square with those identified in other research, but this study does not link them to student outcomes.

Brookover, W. B., & Lezotte, L. W. (1979). *Changes in school characteristics coincident with changes in student achievement.* East Lansing: College of Urban Development, Michigan State University. (ERIC Document Reproduction Service No. ED181005)

Investigates the reasons for achievement increases in six low-SES urban elementary schools and for achievement decreases in two such schools. Identifies an array of effective schooling practices for improving schools.

Bulach, C., Boothe, D., & Michael, P. (1999, April). *Supervisory behaviors that affect school climate.* Paper presented at the annual meeting of the American Educational Research Association, Montreal, Quebec, Canada. (ERIC Document Reproduction Service No. ED430282)

Assesses teachers' judgments about their principal's involvement in activities shown to be related to the supervisory climate in a school. A 52-item survey addressing the areas of trust/decision making, control, instructional leadership, human relations, and conflict was completed by 208 teachers. One key finding: Female principals received significantly higher instructional leadership ratings than male principals.

Bulach, C., Lunenburg, F. C., & McCallon, R. (1994, April). *The influence of the principal's leadership style on school climate and student achievement.* Paper presented at the annual meeting of the American Educational Research Association, New Orleans. (ERIC Document Reproduction Service No. ED374506)

Studies data on principals' leadership styles in relation to student achievement and several school climate variables. Principals and teachers in 20 Kentucky elementary schools completed survey instruments. Few relationships were found, indicating that positive achievement outcomes and school climate may result from different leadership styles. One significant finding: Schools whose principals exhibited a "promoter" leadership style (socially outgoing, friendly, imaginative, and vigorous) had higher levels of parent/community involvement.

Butler, L. A. (1997, May). Building on a dream of success. *Principal, 76*(5), 28–31.

Provides a principal's perspective on the leadership behaviors that enabled her to turn her low-performing elementary school into a higher-performing one. These include setting specific and ambitious goals, keeping a consistent focus on raising achievement, increasing—and convincing teachers to increase—expectations of students, integrating the curriculum, using student performance data to plan instruction, and supporting teachers' learning and experimentation.

Cash, J. (1997, November–December). What good leaders do. *Thrust for Educational Leadership, 27*(3), 22–25.

Presents observations on leadership by Jeanie Cash, California's National Distinguished Principal for 1997. Among the traits she believes good leaders have are optimism, the ability to inspire others, creativity, and the ability to give gifts, specifically those identified by Deal and Peterson (1995): love, authorship, power, and significance. She also believes that good leaders "create an environment of trust, commitment, and fun," and that they take care of themselves so as to be able to do all the above-mentioned things.

Charles, G. S., & Karr-Kidwell, P. J. (1995). *Effective principals, effective schools: Arriving at site-based decision-making with successful principals and teacher participation.* Denton: Texas Woman's University. (ERIC Document Reproduction Service No. ED382564)

Uses feedback on a teacher survey to make recommendations to principals who hope to achieve success by implementing site-based decision making in their schools. The number of survey respondents was quite small, which limits the ability to generalize from the findings.

Chase, C. M., & Kane, M. B. (1983). *The principal as instructional leader: How much more time before we act?* Denver, CO: Education Commission of the States, Task Force on Education for Economic Growth. (ERIC Document Reproduction Service No. ED244369)

Reviews research on principals—how they relate to others in the school, how they manage their time, and what characteristics are common to effective principals. The researchers found that effective principals share several characteristics: establishing a vision, setting clear instructional goals, focusing on continuous improvement, maintaining an orderly and positive learning environment, allocating resources to support goals, setting high standards and expectations for teachers and students, and being confident in their ability to bring about change.

Cheng, Y. C. (1994). Principal's leadership as a critical factor for school performance: Evidence from multi-levels of primary schools. *School Effectiveness and School Improvement, 5*(3), 299–317.

Uses data from the large-scale Education Quality in Hong Kong Primary Schools Study to identify relationships among principals' leadership, school organizational characteristics, teachers' performance, and several student affective outcome measures. The strength of principals' leadership is strongly related to organizational characteristics and teachers' performance, and moderately related to student outcomes.

Cotton, K. (1992). *School-based management.* (Topical Synthesis No. 6). Portland, OR: Northwest Regional Educational Laboratory.

Reviews research on school-based management and identifies the conditions under which it improves school decision making and those under which it fails to do so. Emphasizes the importance of broadly shared decision making at the school level and the need for training school-based management teams. Offers recommendations to states, districts, and schools based on findings.

Cotton, K. (2000). *The schooling practices that matter most.* Alexandria, VA: Association for Supervision and Curriculum Development.

Identifies and describes 15 elements of school context and instructional practice that researchers have found to be most critical to the learning success of all children. Includes a representative bibliography of school- and teacher-effects research from the 1970s onward.

Couch, J. C. (1991, November). *A study of student achievement and how it relates to the principal in the role of instructional leader.* Paper presented at the annual meeting of the Mid-South Educational Research Association, Lexington, KY. (ERIC Document Reproduction Service No. ED340136)

Examines data on Mississippi principals, teachers, and eighth graders in 104 schools to explore the relationship between principals' instructional leadership and student achievement. Researchers attributed their failure to find any relationship to the way the study was structured, that is, "amount of time spent on duties directly related to instructional leadership" (p. 19) may not be the best indicator of the principal's instructional leadership role.

Coyle, L. M., & Witcher, A. E. (1992). Transforming the idea into actions: Policies and practices to enhance school effectiveness. *Urban Education, 26*(4), 390–400.

Summarizes the findings of numerous research efforts that have sought to identify the key features of effective schools. These are mainly congruent with those identified in other summaries of this nature and include emphasis on the role of the principal as instructional leader, disciplinarian, role model for staff and students, and chief architect and promoter of a shared vision for the school.

Davis, S. H. (1998, November–December). Taking aim at effective leadership. *Thrust for Educational Leadership, 28*(2), 6–9.
Draws upon research to identify personal attributes, behaviors, and organizational outcomes related to principals' effective school leadership. Among the correlates identified are intelligence; internal locus of control; self-reflection; willingness to seek acceptance; people skills; decisiveness; task orientation; organization; the establishment of a positive climate; the ability to mobilize support in pursuit of goals; student achievement; and parent, community, and student attitudes.

DeBevoise, W. (1984, February). Synthesis of research on the principal as instructional leader. *Educational Leadership, 41*(5), 14–20.

Summarizes findings from studies on the nature of the principal's instructional leadership functions and the relationship between these functions and student achievement. This classic report both identifies instructional leadership behaviors related to student achievement and emphasizes that different kinds of leadership styles can be effective.

Delaney, J. G. (1997, February). Principal leadership: A primary factor in school-based management and school improvement. *NASSP Bulletin, 81*(586), 107–111.

Reports on research that used a case study approach to determine which leadership behaviors in principals lead to school improvement. Respondents emphasized shared decision making, consensus building, communication skills, and coalition building, but they also favored principals who are strong and inspiring leaders.

Eagly, A. H., Karau, S. J., & Johnson, B. T. (1992, February). Gender and leadership style among school principals: A meta-analysis. *Educational Administration Quarterly, 28*(1), 76–102.

Reviews 50 studies comparing the leadership styles of public school principals and finds that female principals scored higher than males on task-oriented measures, but about the same on interpersonal measures. Females generally adopt a more democratic or participative style.

Edmonds, R. (1979, October). Effective schools for the urban poor. *Educational Leadership, 37*(1), 15–24.

Reviews research that convincingly demonstrates that poor minority students in urban settings can be successfully educated if supportive attitudes and educational practices are in place. Concludes that strong administrative leadership, a primary focus on learning, an orderly environment, the application of resources to educational priority areas, and frequent monitoring of student progress are essential for serving these children effectively.

Evans, L., & Teddlie, C. (1995). Facilitating change in schools: Is there one best style? *School Effectiveness and School Improvement, 6*(1), 1–22.

Reviews literature on effective principal behaviors and provides results of a study of 472 teachers in 53 schools to determine relationships among principals' styles of facilitating change, school SES, and school effectiveness. One of the findings was that effective low-SES schools were more likely to have strong, assertive "initiator"-style principals than ineffective low-SES schools were. The researchers conclude that different facilitation styles might be appropriate for different school contexts.

Firestone, W. A., & Wilson, B. L. (1989). *Administrative behavior, school SES, and student achievement: A preliminary investigation.* Philadelphia, PA: Research for Better Schools. (ERIC Document Reproduction Service No. ED374563)

Uses data from nearly 300 elementary and secondary schools in Pennsylvania to identify relationships among family SES, principal and teacher influence, and teachers' perceptions of student achievement. Key findings include: principals' support of teachers' management of instruction is positively related to achievement at both levels, tight administrative control over teaching is negatively related to achievement, and principals in lower-SES schools exercise tighter control than those in higher-SES schools do.

Gantner, M. W. (1997). *A study of parental views regarding the characteristics of an effective school leader.* El Paso: Department of Educational Leadership & Foundations, University of Texas at El Paso. (ERIC Document Reproduction Service No. ED420103)

Presents outcomes of a series of focus groups with parents in the El Paso area, who identified qualities they felt it important for school principals to possess. Parents' strongest desires were that principals love children, communicate high expectations for their learning ability, and value parents' input into decision making. Participants were from all socioeconomic levels, included Anglo, black, and Hispanic parents, and consisted both of English-speaking parents and those who speak only Spanish.

Gantner, M. W., Daresh, J. C., Dunlap, K., & Newsom, J. (1999, April). *Effective school leadership attributes: Voices from the field.* Paper presented at the annual meeting of the American Educational Research Association, Quebec, Montreal, Canada. (ERIC Document Reproduction Service No. ED431226)

Presents results of focus-group sessions with teachers, parents, and students and individual interviews with school board members in the El Paso, Texas, school district regarding the most desirable leadership attributes for school principals. School board members valued technical managerial skills, but parents, teachers, and students emphasized communication and positive human relationships.

Gaziel, H. (1995). Managerial work patterns of principals at high- and average-performing Israeli elementary schools. *The Elementary School Journal, 96*(2), 179–194.

Compares the work behaviors of principals in high-performing schools with those of principals in schools whose performance is average. Finds many similarities but some notable differences, especially the greater amounts of time spent on instructional management, school improvement, and parent/community relations by principals of high-performing schools. Offers recommendations based on findings.

Glasman, N. S. (1984, Fall). Student achievement and the school principal. *Educational Evaluation and Policy Analysis, 6*(3), 283–296.

Reviews literature on links between schooling factors and student achievement and uses findings from an exploratory study to design an approach to studying principals' use of student performance data to bring about improvements in student performance.

Glover, D., Levacic, R., Bennett, N., & Earley, P. (1996). Leadership, planning and resource management in four very effective schools. Part 1: Setting the scene. *School Organisation, 16*(2), 135–148.

Profiles four secondary schools in terms of the management styles of their "headteachers" (principals) and the relationships between the schools and the environments in which they operate. That all four schools are high-achieving, despite differences in leadership style and ways of interacting with their communities, suggests that both participatory and authoritarian management can be successful.

Gullatt, D. E., & Lofton, B. D. (1996, December). *The principal's role in promoting academic gain.* Natchitoches: Northwestern State University of Louisiana, Alexandria: Rapides Parish School Board. (ERIC Document Reproduction Service No. ED403227)

Reviews and summarizes literature about the effects of principals' behaviors on student achievement. Of particular interest was their approach to (1) governing the school, (2) building collaborative linkages, and (3) organizing and allocating professional work time. Findings are congruent with those emerging from other major reviews on the principal behavior–student achievement relationship.

Gurr, D. (1997). *Principal leadership: What does it do, what does it look like?* Melbourne, Australia: Department of Education Policy and Management, University of Melbourne. Available: http://www.apcentre.edu.au/respapers/gurrd.html

Summarizes literature on the leadership role of the principal, the effects of the principal's leadership on student outcomes, and speculation about the principal's leadership role in the future. Concurs with other contemporary researchers that the principal's influence on student outcomes is considerable, but achieved indirectly, through the work of others.

Hallinger, P., Bickman, L., & Davis, K. (1989, March). *What makes a difference? School context, principal leadership, and student achievement.* Paper presented at the annual meeting of the American Educational Research Association, San Francisco. (ERIC Document Reproduction Service No. ED308578)

Reports on the same study as Hallinger, Bickman, & Davis, 1996.

Hallinger, P., Bickman, L., & Davis, K. (1996, May). School context, principal leadership, and student reading achievement. *The Elementary School Journal, 96*(5), 527–549.

Uses data from a sample of 87 Tennessee elementary schools to determine relationships among school context variables, the instructional leadership behaviors of principals, and the reading achievement of children in grades three and six. Analysis yielded findings about contextual effects *on* principals' leadership, as well as findings about the effects *of* principals' instructional leadership on student achievement through mediating variables, specifically those associated with establishing a clear school mission.

Hallinger, P., & Heck, R. H. (1996, February). Reassessing the principal's role in school effectiveness: A review of empirical research, 1980–1995. *Educational Administration Quarterly, 32*(1), 5–44.

Reviews research on whether principals' behaviors affect student outcomes, particularly academic achievement, and by what means this occurs. Examination of 40 studies reveals that many study designs do not provide useful answers to these questions. Studies with the best conceptual frameworks and methodologies indicate that the principals' effects on student outcomes are indirect, mediated via those who have more frequent contact with students.

Heck, R. H. (1992, Spring). Principals' instructional leadership and school performance: Implications for policy development. *Educational Evaluation and Policy Analysis, 14*(1), 21–34.

Reports results from a large-scale outlier study and offers cautions about holding principals accountable for school performance. Findings about the difference between principals' instructional leadership at the elementary and secondary levels are reported, along with findings concerning the difficulties involved in bringing about change in low-performing schools. The study did, however, identify several principal behaviors that are closely related to high achievement.

Heck, R. H. (1993). School context, principal leadership, and achievement: The case of secondary schools in Singapore. *The Urban Review, 25*(2), 151–166.

Identifies relationships among indicators of school context, principals' leadership behaviors, and student achievement as determined through surveys with 156 high-, average-, and low-achieving secondary school teachers in Singapore. High-achieving schools were perceived as exhibiting greater democracy, teamwork, teacher influence in decision making, protection from external problems by their principals, and greater principal understanding of school problems.

Heck, R. H., Larsen, T. J., & Marcoulides, G. A. (1990, May). Instructional leadership and school achievement: Validation of a causal model. *Educational Administration Quarterly, 26*(2), 94–125.

Presents a causal model of the manner in which principals influence student achievement through their instructional leadership behaviors. The model was developed based on the work of many researchers. Schools with higher-than-average achievement and those with lower-than-average achievement were examined and found to fit the model postulated.

Heck, R. H., & Marcoulides, G. A. (1993, May). Principal leadership behaviors and school achievement. *NASSP Bulletin, 77*(553), 20–28.

Compares survey responses of principals and teachers from two categories of schools—those with above-average achievement for their demographic profile and those with achievement below demographically similar schools. Ratings on 17 instructional leadership indicators revealed that principals of higher-achieving schools exhibit more instructional leadership behaviors. No differences were noted between elementary and secondary schools.

High, R. M., & Achilles, C. M. (1986, April). *Principal influence in instructionally effective schools.* Paper presented at the annual meeting of the American Educational Research Association, San Francisco. (ERIC Document Reproduction Service No. ED277115)

Examines four high-achieving and six fairly effective elementary and middle schools in terms of the influence-gaining behaviors exhibited by the schools' principals. Those from the high-achieving schools exhibited greater use of the available power bases—exercising legitimate authority, knowledge, and expertise; norm setting; involving others in decision making; using coercion; applying interpersonal knowledge; and extending rewards.

Hipp, K. A. (1996, April). *Teacher efficacy: Influence of principal leadership behavior.* Paper presented at the annual meeting of the American Educational Research Association, New York. (ERIC Document Reproduction Service No. ED396409)

Explores the relationships between principals' leadership behaviors and teacher efficacy in 10 middle schools in Wisconsin attempting to change. Data were collected through surveys and interviews with teachers and principals. Analysis of the data identified 11 behaviors related to both general and personal teacher efficacy, including providing personal and professional support, promoting teacher empowerment and decision making, and fostering teamwork and collaboration.

Johnson, J. F., & Asera, R. (1999). *Hope for urban education: A study of nine high-performing, high-poverty, urban elementary schools.* Austin: Charles A. Dana Center, University of Texas. Available: http://www.ed.gov/pubs/urbanhope/title

Reports on a study of nine high-performing elementary schools serving children of color in poor urban communities. Researchers identified both unique characteristics and commonalities across the schools; among the latter were leaders' goal orientation, their ability to mobilize staff in support of children's needs, their fostering of a positive school climate, their support of teachers' focus on instructional issues, and their provision of professional development resources and opportunities.

Johnson, N. A., & Holdaway, E. A. (1991). Perceptions of effectiveness and the satisfaction of principals in elementary schools. *The Journal of Educational Administration, 29*(1), 51–70.

Examines 112 Canadian principals and their perceptions of their effectiveness, their job satisfaction, the effectiveness of their schools, and the perceptions of superintendents and teachers regarding the principals' effectiveness. Many relationships were identified, but school effectiveness was *not* determined by principals' job satisfaction, or vice versa. Overall effectiveness of principals and overall effectiveness of schools *were* highly correlated.

Kirby, P. C., Paradise, L. V., & King, M. I. (1992, May–June). Extraordinary leaders in education: Understanding transformational leadership. *Journal of Educational Research, 85*(5), 301–311.

Reports results of two studies that looked at administrator attributes in relation to satisfaction and perceived effectiveness. Key finding: While the positive effects of leaders were sometimes ascribed to their personal traits, they were more often attributed to specific behaviors, such as modeling the attitudes and behaviors they expect of staff, communicating high expectations and challenging followers, involving others in goal setting, and providing professional development opportunities.

Krug, S. E. (1992). *Instructional leadership, school instructional climate, and student learning outcomes. Project report.* Urbana, IL: National Center for School Leadership, MetriTech, Inc. (ERIC Document Reproduction Service No. ED359668)

Compares principal, teacher, and student data from 77 elementary and middle schools in suburban Chicago. Data included student achievement and attitudes, along with principals' self-assessments on instructional leadership and principals' and teachers' assessment of the instructional climate. Key finding: a significantly positive correlation was noted between principals' self-ratings on instructional leadership and the student outcomes of academic satisfaction, recognition, accomplishment, and commitment.

Larsen, J. J. (1987, April). *Identification of instructional leadership behaviors and the impact of their implementation on academic achievement.* Paper presented at the annual meeting of the American Educational Research Association, Washington, D.C. (ERIC Document Reproduction Service No. ED281286)

To develop a principal and teacher survey, the author used a validated list of instructional leadership behaviors that were considered most important. The survey was administered in 76 high- and low-achieving California elementary schools. Compared to teachers in low-performing schools, teachers in high-performing schools gave their principals significantly higher frequency-of-performance ratings on items in six instructional leadership areas: goal setting, school/community relations, supervision and evaluation, school climate, coordination, and staff development.

Leithwood, K., & Jantzi, D. (1999, December). Transformational school leadership effects: A replication. *School Effectiveness and School Improvement, 10*(4), 451–479.

Replicates a previous study by the same authors of the effects of transformational leadership on organizational conditions and student engagement as measured by participation in school activities and self-reports on feelings of connectedness with school. Transformational leadership has significant effects on both outcome areas.

Leithwood, K. A., & Montgomery, D. J. (1982, Fall). The role of the elementary school principal in program improvement. *Review of Educational Research, 52*(3), 309–339.

Reviews research on effective elementary principals, as contrasted with typical principals, with regard to actions taken to improve instructional programs. Effective principals were

94

found to be actively involved with teachers and with the instructional program in a variety of ways, while typical principals were not, being, instead, "drowned in a sea of administrivia" (p. 330).

Leitner, D. (1994). Do principals affect student outcomes: An organizational perspective. *School Effectiveness and School Improvement, 5*(3), 219–238.

Reports on a study of relationships among principals' instructional management behaviors, students' socioeconomic backgrounds, and student achievement in 27 elementary schools. Finds that principals' effects on student achievement are indirect and complex, being mediated through principal-teacher interactions. Based on his findings, the author cautions against holding simplistic notions of the principal-student achievement relationship.

Levine, D. U., & Levine, R. F. (2000). *Two routes to unusual effectiveness.* Unpublished manuscript, University of Nebraska, Omaha.

Reports findings from studies of four schools where student performance significantly exceeds that of most schools with similar characteristics. Findings are organized under four key characteristics—unusually effective organizational arrangements for low achievers, emphasis on central learning skills and higher-order learning, appropriate monitoring of student progress, and "doability"/manageability.

Manasse, A. L. (1984, February). Principals as leaders of high-performing systems. *Educational Leadership, 41*(5), 42–46.

Cites research findings in support of the idea that effective principals are more like leaders of high-performing systems than like ordinary principals. Notes such similarities as being proactive rather than reactive, pushing the organization to achieve their vision, possessing the analytical and interpersonal skills to move others toward the organization's goals, and using such things as symbols and slogans to inspire staff and constituents.

McCallum, B. (1999). Literacy in four effective schools. *School Leadership & Management, 19*(1), 7–24.

Examines practices in four British primary schools with high literacy achievement to identify commonalities among them. Fifteen attributes were identified. Key behaviors of headteachers (principals) were identified in some of these attributes and "their 'hand' is detected" (p. 23) in all of them. The instructional leadership of headteachers is identified as a key factor in the schools' success.

Mendez-Morse, S. (1991, Summer). The principal's role in the instructional process: Implications for at-risk students. *Issues . . . about Change, 1*(3).

Examines and summarizes research that has identified the instructional leadership behaviors of principals in schools where at-risk students are exhibiting high achievement. Distinguishes between managers, who oversee operations and maintain the status quo, and leaders, who foster change in the direction of a vision for improvement of the organization.

Ortiz, F. I., & Marshall, C. (1988). Women in educational administration. In N. Boyan (Ed.), *Handbook of research on educational administration* (pp. 123–141). White Plains, NY: Longman.

Addresses the history of the organization and management of schools throughout this century and the issues of gender and power that have arisen in response to the structures that have evolved. Compares and contrasts men and women in the principal's role and finds more democratic leadership on the part of women.

Pavan, B. N., & Reid, N. A. (1994, January). Effective urban elementary schools and their women administrators. *Urban Education, 28*(4), 425–438.

Notes that four of the five highest-performing Chapter 1 schools in Philadelphia had female principals and studied the behaviors of those principals in light of research on effective schools. Found that the traits linked to successful schools are more commonly found in female principals than in their male counterparts—especially instructional leadership activities and establishment of supportive climates.

Peterson, K. D., Gok, K., & Warren, V. D. (1995, August). *Principals' skills and knowledge for shared decision making.* Madison: Center on Organization and Restructuring of Schools, University of Wisconsin-Madison. (ERIC Document Reproduction Service No. ED386827)

Reports findings from a study of 24 schools implementing site-based, shared decision-making processes. The process was poorly managed in many sites, but researchers found that successful principals (1) communicated a clear educational vision, (2) had effective structures and practices for decision making, and (3) established work teams and worked effectively with them.

Reavis, C. A., Vinson, D., & Fox, R. (1999, March–April). Importing a culture of success via a strong principal. *Clearing House, 72*(4), 199–201.

Provides results of a year-long case study of a predominantly minority high school in Texas that quickly soared from below average to highly successful under the guidance of a new principal. Discusses the principal's activities in light of research on successful schools.

Reitzug, U. C. (1997, Summer). Images of principal instructional leadership: From supervision to collaborative inquiry. *Journal of Curriculum and Supervision, 12*(4), 356–366.

Begins with the observation that most textbooks on supervision present it as the principal's main instructional leadership function. Reviews 10 supervision textbooks used in principal preparation programs and finds their portrayal of principals, teachers, teaching, and supervision itself to be at odds with researchers' findings about effective ways for principals and teachers to work together. Offers suggestions based on findings.

Renchler, R. (1992, February). *Student motivation, school culture, and academic achievement: What school leaders can do.* Trends & Issues Paper. Eugene, OR: ERIC Clearinghouse on Educational Management. (ERIC Reproduction Service No. ED351741)

Reviews research on the psychology of motivation and the relationship of motivation to school culture, pedagogical practice, and school restructuring. Concludes that lack of motivation on the part of students is widespread. Translates key research findings into recommendations that principals can use to increase teacher and student motivation, thereby improving student performance.

Riordan, G., & da Costa, J. L. (1998, April). *Leadership for effective teacher collaboration: Suggestions for principals and teacher leaders.* Paper presented at the annual meeting of the American

Educational Research Association, San Diego, CA. (ERIC Document Reproduction Service No. ED418964)

Provides overviews of five studies that explore different aspects of teacher collaboration. After reporting their findings that effective teacher collaboration is linked to higher student performance, the authors describe elements of effective collaboration, identify common barriers to achieving it, and offer recommendations to help administrators foster successful collaborations among their staffs.

Sagor, R. D. (1992, February). Three principals who make a difference. *Educational Leadership, 49*(5), 13–18.

Profiles three principals of high-performing, continuously improving schools to identify the commonalities that underlie their different leadership styles. A clear focus, a common cultural perspective, and a constant push for improvement characterized the leadership approach of all three principals and the schools they led.

Sammons, P., Hillman, J., & Mortimore, P. (1995, April). *Key characteristics of effective schools: A review of school effectiveness research.* London: Institute of Education. (ERIC Document Reproduction Service No. ED389826)

Reviews a very large body of research on effective schooling and distills characteristics that are reliably found in schools with high student achievement. Practices in 11 areas are identified and defined, including professional leadership, shared vision and goals, a positive learning environment, concentration on teaching and learning, purposeful teaching, high expectations, positive reinforcement, progress monitoring, pupil rights and responsibilities, home-school partnership, and functioning as a learning organization.

Sammons, P., Thomas, S., Mortimore, P., Walker, A., Cairns, C., & Bausor, J. (1998). Understanding differences in academic effectiveness: Practitioners' views. *School Effectiveness and School Improvement, 9*(3), 286–309.

From a study of 94 British secondary schools, draws a group of six outliers—two effective, two ineffective, and two mixed—for in-depth case studies. "Headteachers" (principals) and their deputies were questioned about an array of factors that bear on school effectiveness. Results are congruent with the generally accepted findings about effectiveness, including the importance of the leader's creativity and ability to communicate and to get input from staff for decision making.

Scarnati, J. T. (1994, April). Beyond technical competence: Nine rules for administrators. *NASSP Bulletin, 78*(561), 76–83.

From his perspective as a junior-senior high school principal in New York, the author offers his convictions about the character attributes that principals need in addition to "technical competence" in instructional and business management. Draws heavily upon the leadership literature and his experience in military service to advance his arguments.

Scheurich, J. J. (1998, November). Highly successful and loving, public elementary schools populated mainly by low-SES children of color: Core beliefs and cultural characteristics. *Urban Education, 33*(4), 451–491.

Uses the direct experience of the author and his doctoral students with high-performing elementary schools serving poor children of color as a point of departure for developing a schooling model to better serve poor minority children in general. A key data source is principals who have transformed low-performing schools with these demographics into high-performing schools.

Shakeshaft, C. (1989). *Women in educational administration.* Newbury Park, CA: Sage.

Discusses historical and current issues regarding female administrators, including barriers they have faced, strategies for overcoming them, and the need for more inclusive theory and practice. Cites research contrasting the leadership behavior of male and female administrators. Concludes that female educational administrators need not emulate the approaches to leadership taken by their male counterparts to be successful.

Short, P. M., & Spencer, W. A. (1990, Winter). Principal instructional leadership. *Journal of Research and Development in Education, 23*(2), 117–122.

Compares teacher perceptions of principals' instructional leadership with student perceptions of classroom variables in 16 secondary schools. Among several correlations noted was that, in schools where principals were seen as effective in communicating goals and active in supervising and evaluating instruction, students were cooperative and helpful toward each other. Also, active instructional leadership by the principal correlated positively with highly motivated and engaged students and negatively with levels of classroom competition.

Silins, H. C. (1992, December). Effective leadership for school reform. *The Alberta Journal of Educational Research, 38*(4), 317–334.

Examines the relationship between types of school leadership and school improvement outcomes to determine whether transformational or transactional leadership approaches better explain the outcomes noted. Examination of survey responses from 679 Canadian teachers indicated that transformational leadership (which focuses on transcending personal needs), was positively related to effects on school, program and instruction, and students. Transactional leadership (which focuses on self-interest) was positively related to teacher effects only.

Silins, H. C. (1994, April). *Leadership characteristics that make a difference to schools.* Paper presented at the annual meeting of the American Educational Research Association, New Orleans. (ERIC Document Reproduction Service No. ED383086)

Reports results of a survey of 291 Australian primary (elementary) teachers on a variety of transactional and transformational leadership characteristics. The two areas that had a perceived positive effect on student performance were *goal achievement* (sense of purpose and organizational mission; engaging others in pursuit of positive change) and *ethos* (building shared values, expectations, and behaviors that collectively make up a school's culture).

Sizemore, B. (1985). Pitfalls and promises of effective schools research. *Journal of Negro Education, 54*(3), 269–288.

Draws upon observations and interviews in schools in Pittsburgh to identify practices related to the high achievement of African American children from poor families. Identifies an array of organizational factors and principal behaviors that are positively related to students' achievement. Notably, the successful principals believe in the high learning capability of their students and organize the school to support high levels of learning.

Steller, A. W. (1988). *Effective schools research: Practice and promise.* Fastback 276. Bloomington, IN: Phi Delta Kappa Educational Foundation. (ERIC Document Reproduction Service No. ED299698)

Reviews the research on effective schooling practices and identifies combinations of variables identified across many studies and reviews as essential to school effectiveness. The section focusing on principals emphasizes the importance of instructional leadership and identifies its components.

Stolp, S. (1991). *Leadership for school culture.* ERIC Digest #91. Eugene, OR. (ERIC Clearinghouse on Educational Management, No. ED370198)

Identifies a relationship between positive school culture and increases in student achievement, the components of school culture, and actions principals can take to improve school culture and, therefore, student achievement.

Teddlie, C., & Reynolds, D. (2000). *The international handbook of school effectiveness research.* London: Falmer.

Reviews the international research evidence on what constitutes effective schooling and how we can bring what we know to bear on improving schools, especially those in greatest need. Analyzes relationships among school effects research, teacher effects research, and school improvement efforts. Emphasizes the importance of principals' knowledge and support of the instructional program.

Thomas, V. (1997). *What research says about administrators' management style, effectiveness, and teacher morale.* Chicago: Chicago State University. (ERIC Document Reproduction Service No. ED411569)

Reviews a large body of literature on principals' leadership and the direct and indirect outcomes of different leadership approaches. A democratic, collaborative, and transformational approach to leadership has the most positive effects on teacher morale and performance, and high teacher morale has a beneficial effect on student achievement.

Valentine, J. W., & Bowman, M. L. (1991, December). Effective principal, effective school: Does research support the assumption? *NASSP Bulletin, 75*(539), 1–7.

Compares the perceptions of two groups of teachers regarding the effectiveness of their principals—teachers from schools selected as effective through the national School Recognition Program and those from randomly selected schools. Principals of the recognized schools received higher ratings across the board than those from the randomly selected schools and received especially high ratings in the areas of providing organizational direction, utilizing effective interactive processes, and establishing/using organizational linkages.

VanderStoep, S. W., Anderman, E. M., & Midgley, C. (1994). The relationship among principal 'venturesomeness,' a stress on excellence, and the personal engagement of teachers and students. *School Effectiveness and School Improvement, 5*(3), 254–271.

Reveals outcomes of two studies conducted with approximately 3,000 students in grades 3–5 in Arizona and Florida. The studies were intended to test a model of the relationship among (1) how venturesome a principal is, (2) whether a school's culture is accomplishment oriented, (3) how professionally committed teachers are, and (4) how committed students are to school and to learning. Researchers present the puzzling finding that teacher and student commitment are unrelated and discuss reasons for this finding.

Wagstaff, M., Melton, J., Lasless, B., & Combs, L. (1998). *African-American student achievement research project*. Kilgore, TX: Region VII Education Service Center. (ERIC Document Reproduction Service No. ED425256)

Reports results of a study of three high-performing Texas school districts with high proportions of African American students. The purpose was to identify the achievement-enhancing practices at those districts in hopes of helping lower-performing districts improve. The activities of the principals in the high-performing districts are typical of those identified in other successful school environments.

Walberg, H. J., & Lane, J. J. (1985). The role of the administrator in school productivity. *Studies in Educational Evaluation, 11,* 217–230.

Reviews research on the factors closely associated with student learning and discusses the areas where principals have—or do not have—influence over these factors. Makes research-based recommendations that can help principals to improve student achievement in their schools.

Wendel, F. C., Hoke, F. A., & Joekel, R. G. (1996). *Outstanding school administrators: Their keys to success*. Westport, CT: Praeger.

Solicits a wealth of information from 491 school administrators identified by their colleagues as "outstanding." Organizes their perceptions under the headings of educational philosophy, values, visionary leadership, institutional leadership, commitment, interpersonal relations, innovation and quality, risk taking, communication, selection, and personal development and professional organizations.

Zigarelli, M. A. (1996, November–December). An empirical test of conclusions from effective schools research. *Journal of Educational Research, 90*(2), 103–110.

Uses three years' worth of data from the National Educational Longitudinal Study to identify relationships between the classic "effective schools" correlates and student achievement. Found that relatively few such correlates were related to student performance.

ABOUT THE AUTHOR

Kathleen Cotton was a Research Associate with the School Improvement Program of the Northwest Regional Educational Laboratory (NWREL) and the author or coauthor of more than 70 publications. From 1987 to 1996, she coordinated the development of the School Improvement Research Series, a collection of syntheses of educational research literature on topics of current interest and feature articles showcasing exemplary school programs from around the United States. Her research summaries identified effective practices in many topic areas, including citizenship education, employ-ability skills, the education of urban minority youth, thinking skills, schoolwide and classroom discipline, early childhood education, and parent involvement.

Cotton also published papers on the effects of school size, teacher expectations, multi-age grouping, and other topics. She authored a general research synthesis and a best practices synthesis, as well as two books copublished by NWREL and ASCD: *Research You Can Use to Improve Results* (1999) and *The Schooling Practices That Matter Most* (2000). She has been quoted about her research on school size in dozens of U.S. newspapers, as well as *Time* magazine and the *Utne Reader.* Her B.A. from the University of Oregon and M.A. from Portland State University were both in English.

Related ASCD Resources

Principals and Student Achievement: What the Research Says

At the time of publication, the following ASCD resources were available; for the most up-to-date information about ASCD resources, go to www.ascd.org. ASCD stock numbers are noted in parentheses.

Audiotapes

Benchmark Schools Study: High Achievement Results with Special Populations of Students by Gordon Cawelti (#298076)

No Excuses: Closing the Achievement Gap (2 tapes) by Patricia Davenport (#203172) **ALSO ON CD!**

Dropping Out of the Principalship: Why Are We Losing High School Administrators and What Can We Do About It? by Angela Spaulding and Mick Stevens (#201167)

Facilitating Data-Driven School Improvement by Jan O'Neill and Linda D'Acquisto (#202174)

The Principal's Role in Building a Professional Learning Community by Ricard DuFour (#200259)

Multimedia

Guiding School Improvement with Action Research Books-in-Action Package (10 copies of *Guiding School Improvement with Action Research,* by Richard Sagor, and 1 video) (#700261)

Promoting Learning Through Student Data Professional Inquiry Kit by Marian Leibowitz (8 activity folders and 1 videotape). (#999004)

Networks

Visit the ASCD Web site (www.ascd.org) and search for "networks" for information about professional educators who have formed groups around topics like "Basic School," "Higher Education and K–12 in Service of Teaching and Learning," and "Instructional Supervision." Look in the "Network Directory" for current facilitators' addresses and phone numbers.

Online Resources

Visit ASCD's Web site (www.ascd.org) for the following professional development opportunities:

Educational Leadership: Using Data to Improve Student Achievement (entire issue, February 2003) Excerpted articles online free; entire issue online and accessible to ASCD members (#103031)

Educational Topics: *School Culture/Climate* (free)

Journal of Curriculum and Supervision (Vol. 14, Summer 1999) Excerpted articles online free; entire issue online and accessible to ASCD members (#199022)

Professional Development Online: *Effective Leadership* by Frank Betts, among others (for a small fee; password protected)

Print Products

Closing the Achievement Gap: A Vision for Changing Beliefs and Practices, 2nd Edition, edited by Belinda Williams (#102010) **NEW!**

Enhancing Student Achievement: A Framework for School Improvement by Charlotte Danielson (#102109)

Leadership Capacity for Lasting School Improvement by Linda Lambert (#102283) **NEW!**

Motivating Students and Teachers in an Era of Standards by Richard Sagor (#103009) **NEW!**

Professional Learning Communities at Work: Best Practices for Enhancing Student Achievement by Richard DuFour and Robert Eaker (#198188)

The Results Fieldbook: Practical Strategies from Dramatically Improved Schools by Mike Schmoker (#101001)

Student Achievement Through Staff Development, 3rd Edition, by Bruce Joyce and Beverly Showers (#102003)

What Works in Schools: Translating Research into Action by Robert J. Marzano (#102271)

Videos

The Principal Series (7 videos with 2 facilitator's guides) Educational consultants: Richard DuFour and Karen Dyer (#499242)

What Works in Schools Video Series (3 videos) Educational consultant: Robert J. Marzano (#403047)

For more information, visit us on the World Wide Web (http://www.ascd.org), send an e-mail message to member@ascd.org, call the ASCD Service Center (1-800-933-ASCD or 703-578-9600, then press 2), send a fax to 703-575-5400, or write to Information Services, ASCD, 1703 N. Beauregard St., Alexandria, VA 22311-1714 USA.